Ernesto 'Che' Guevara

BACK ON THE ROAD

A Journey to Central America

Translated from the Spanish by Patrick Camiller

With an Introduction by Richard Gott
and a Foreword by Alberto Granado

VINTAGE

Published by Vintage 2002

Vintage is grateful to Gianni Mina
for making publication of this work possible

2 4 6 8 10 9 7 5 3 1

Copyright © Archivo Personal del Che 2000
English translation © Patrick Camiller 2001
Introduction © Richard Gott 2001
Foreword © Alberto Granado 2000

First published with the title *Otra vez* in 2000 by
Sperling & Kupfer Editori S.p.A., Milan

This edition first published in Great Britain, by
arrangement with Sperling & Kupfer, in 2001 by
The Harvill Press

Vintage
Random House, 20 Vauxhall Bridge Road,
London SW1V 2SA

Random House Australia (Pty) Limited
20 Alfred Street, Milsons Point, Sydney,
New South Wales 2061, Australia

Random House New Zealand Limited
18 Poland Road, Glenfield
Auckland 10, New Zealand

Random House (Pty) Limited
Endulini, 5A Jubilee Road, Parktown 2193,
South Africa

The Random House Group Limited Reg. No. 954009

www.randomhouse.co.uk

A CIP catalogue record for this book
is available from the British Library

ISBN 1 860 46972 8

Papers used by Random House are natural, recyclable
products made from wood grown in sustainable
forests. The manufacturing processes conform to the
environmental regulations of the country of origin

Printed and bound in Great Britain by
Bookmarque Ltd, Croydon, Surrey

Note to the reader

Back on the Road is a personal text with the character of a testimony, indispensable to get inside the iron-willed personality that Ernesto Guevara de la Serna successfully forged for himself with the written word as his constant accomplice. Irony and humour are interwoven with a deep perception of the surroundings through which he passed in his urge to discover the Americas, offering us a high-quality picture of his own future imbued with thought and action.

Among the antecedents of this diary are the chronicles so full of youthful spirit that he reconstructed after his first trip in Latin America,* which communicate "the joyful impulse . . . that was lost on the horizon of the Americas".

The present diary-notes mark the prelude to his development as a fully formed revolutionary. They could have been written up at the time as a polished account along the lines of the *Motorcycle Diaries*, but that did not happen for reasons which nobody would challenge. Instead, they merit publication as a valuable historical bequest in their own right, testifying to crucial events in his travels through "our great American continent".

To assist the reader's understanding of the text, we have added a number of letters and appendices that make it possible to grasp the full profundity of the young author's reflective and conscientious tone as he embarked on his future life, linked forever with one of the most important events of the twentieth century, the Cuban Revolution.

In Che's eagerness to study his surroundings in depth, his passion for writing always had photography as a vital complement. The volume therefore also contains previously unpublished photographs of his travels, as living testimony of the variety of his experiences and his desire to leave them recorded in images expressing his fine sensitivity and passion to capture everything that excited him.

Archivo Personal del Che

* Ernesto Guevara, *The Motorcycle Diaries: a journey around South America*, London: Verso, 1995, Fourth Estate, 1996

FOREWORD

It is no easy task to write the foreword to a book whose author's work and life made him the paradigm of a human being. For you risk the temptation of transforming him into a myth alien to the reality that surrounded him during his lifetime.

This problem is even greater when the person writing the foreword had the huge good fortune to take part in the conversion of "dream trips" into tangible realities. Those of us who enjoyed his friendship, being close enough to perceive directly the moral and intellectual qualities that set him above the ordinary run of humanity, must always keep remembering that he was only a man and not a mythical being.

With this ideal in mind, I accept the responsibility – as an old friend of his, from as long ago as October 1942 – of introducing his second Latin American travel diary. It is a vivid account in which the reader constantly encounters the flesh-and-blood Ernesto Guevara de la Serna, with all the temerity of his twenty-five years. It shows us the various aspects of a personality still being formed, as he sets out to face all the difficulties of the journey together with his friend Carlos Ferrer (Calica): "two separate wills moving out through the American continent, not knowing the exact aim of their quest nor in which direction lies their objective".

But once he has made the decision to leave the beaten track offered by Venezuela and to discover and participate in the revolution then under way in Guatemala, the change taking place in him becomes more palpable; you can sense his assuredness that he has found the path for which he has been searching.

Whereas his first trip in South America served to deepen his ideas about social distinctions and made him see the importance of struggling against them, this second journey consolidates the political knowledge he has acquired and fuels a growing need for further study to grasp why and how a struggle must be waged that will culminate in a genuine revolution.

With the eyes of remembrance I look back at the leave-taking from his family and friends. They did not understand his reasons yet went through the kind of formal goodbye given to a member of their group or class leaving in search of new horizons – although in this case he was breaking all the group canons and contradicting all the pre-established schemas.

I see him dressed in the "fatigues" of the Argentine Army: tight trousers, rustic shirt, and boots with the laces certainly undone, not as a sign of carelessness, but in keeping with a scale of values in which external show is not the most important.

Hanging from the second-class compartment with a broad smile on his face, holding his half-shaven head straight up (as ever the "closely cropped Guevara"), he pulls out of Buenos Aires station and enters history.

From that moment everything he thought worth noting down appears in the kaleidoscopic pages of the diary, with its constant symbiosis of the literary stylist and the deep-sighted observer.

He gives a graphic description of the countryside around the Bolsa Negra mine in Bolivia and then adds: "But the mine could not be heard throbbing. It lacked the energy of the workers who daily tear their load of materials from the earth, but who were then in La Paz defending the Revolution on this 2nd of August, the Day of the Indian and of the Agrarian Reform."

In this passage we can see tightly compressed what was already becoming axiomatic for Ernesto: the importance of man in all the activities of life. But at the same time it is said with the beauty of a writer of some weight.

Another aspect that strikes one, already in this early diary is the large number of different things that Guevara did during the brief period of his trip. He could, for example, go from giving a lecture on teaching activity at the University of Buenos Aires to speaking about research with the eminent Spanish physiologist P. Suñer, a victim of persecution by the Franco regime.

He had a series of such discussions (and often disagreements) with prominent figures. He drew up a critical balance sheet after each one, and we are astonished at the number of correct insights they contain at a distance of nearly half a century.

When he arrived in Costa Rica he met various exiles, including two who would later play a major political role as presidents of their respective countries. Indeed, his discussions with Juan Bosch from the Dominican Republic and Rómulo Betancourt from Venezuela spontaneously raise the question of how this unknown young man, outwardly unassuming yet incisive and critical in dialogue, could break through the circle of officials that surrounded them. It is not an easy question to answer, but the fact is that he did discuss with them and the conclusions he drew could not have been more accurate.

In a few words he portrays Bosch as he was during his time in government. And he foresees with pitiless realism how Betancourt will later conduct himself, both as president of Venezuela and as head of the Acción Democrática election machine, when he handed over the country's great riches to the United States transnationals.

There is no lack of gaiety and vitality in the diary. Along with the man of ideas, we find a vigorous young man full of energy, sensitive to the presence of women, capable of giving "the negress Socorro" some affection and comfort without betraying himself, and capable too of judging their encounter in its true colours.

The passages describing his time in Mexico are exceptionally important because of the wide range of his interests. He visited museums, admired the murals of Orozco, Rivera, Tamayo and Siqueiros, toured the Aztec pyramids – but without forgetting his true aims. In addition to the fascination of Mexican culture, there is another decisive and irreversible aspect when he writes that he will lead "the life of a proletarian".

And so he does not let himself be tempted by the help offered by Ulises Petit de Murat and his wife, Hilda, Petrona or his own Aunt Beatriz, which would set him on a bourgeois path. He keeps the status of a proletarian, with "the ordinary chain of hopes and disappointments" that characterize the life of that class during the struggle for the capture of real power.

This new attitude to the political problems around him is clearly set out in a discussion with a group of Argentine exiles in Mexico. They want to send a message of support to the new government in Argentina that has sprung up following the overthrow of Perón. But Ernesto asks that, before giving the government their support, they should wait until it has achieved "something definite on such matters as trade union democracy or the running of the economy".

Together with this proletarian consciousness, his great sense of human solidarity swells up more powerfully than ever. Just as, on his first trip, he shared his overcoat with a couple of workers in the freezing night of the Chilean Altiplano, so now in Mexico, despite the hardships he is suffering, he looks for and obtains some money (150 pesos) to help his friend El Patojo return to Guatemala where his mother needs his financial and emotional support.

The final pages perfectly illustrate the three broad lines of action that have marked the first two and a half decades of his life: his interest and talent for science; his wandering among curious travellers and his study of nature and civilizations in the company of friends; and his need to take part in a genuine revolution.

With regard to science, he comments on the presentation in Guanajato of his work on allergy, and weighs the option of doing research work and human medicine.

During these days, when he is writing about his future, he also refers to the idea of meeting the Granados in Caracas – and although he considers it a possibility, it is not so much a firm intention as a fleeting thought and a concession to the urging of his friends. What is especially clear to me is that his way of behaving and thinking is already very different from that of the Fuster with whom he shared some unrepeatable moments in 1952. His desire for travel and research is still there, but you can feel his iron resolve not to become again a semi-scientist, semi-bohemian, semi-revolutionary. Now he is determined to give himself up fully to the great decisive leap.

By one of those accidents of life, it was during this difficult August that he first met Fidel and found in him the strength and support he needed. And if it be said that the diary gives little space to a meeting that was so important for the future, would I be wrong in thinking that as he wrote about it he was paraphrasing for himself the words of the Master, José Martí: Some things must be left in silence . . . ?

Alberto Granado, Havana, August 1998

INTRODUCTION

On 7 July, 1953, at the age of 25 and just graduated as a doctor, Ernesto Guevara climbed into a second-class carriage at the Belgrano railway station in Buenos Aires and headed north for Bolivia and the Andes. Family and friends stood on the platform and waved him goodbye, not without a tear. His mother and father were not to see him again for another six years, when they travelled to Havana in January 1959 at the dawn of the Cuban revolution. By that time their itinerant son had become famous throughout the world as "Che" Guevara, the guerrilla fighter who had fought alongside Fidel Castro to bring revolutionary change to Cuba. Guevara did not himself revisit his homeland until 1961, eight years after he had originally departed.

In the same month that Guevara left Argentina, Castro had already established a small niche for himself in history. On 26 July, 1953, as a fierce and determined opponent of the dictatorship of Fulgencio Batista, recently established the previous year, he had launched an attack on a military barracks at Moncada, in the eastern Cuban city of Santiago. This attempted putsch, made with the object of seizing the armoury in order to provide weapons for his embryonic revolutionary movement, was a dismal failure. More than sixty of his men were gunned down in cold blood, while Castro himself was arrested and sentenced to fifteen years' imprisonment on the Isle of Pines.

Eventually amnestied in May 1955, Castro left Cuba in July for voluntary exile in Mexico City, from where he planned to resume the armed struggle. There he first met Guevara, whose Latin American peregrinations had finally ended up in the Mexican capital. "A political event," Guevara notes drily in his diary, "was that I met Fidel Castro, the Cuban revolutionary. He is a young, intelligent guy, very sure of himself and extraordinarily audacious: I think we hit it off well." The encounter between Castro and Guevara, and their subsequent close friendship and collaboration, was to have a dramatic impact on the history of Latin America in the twentieth century.

Unlike Castro, Guevara had no overt political ambitions when he started on his travels in 1953. He appeared to be embarking on yet another of his indeterminate journeys through the Americas, similar to the one he had made on a motorcycle a year earlier with his fellow medical student Alberto Granado (who has written a foreword to this book). On this second journey he was accompanied initially by another, rather less political, friend from childhood, Carlos Ferrer. Uncertain of his purpose or even of his eventual destination, he had a vague plan to join Granado, who was working at a leprosarium in Venezuela, and an even sketchier notion (common to many middle-class Argentinians of the time) of travelling on to Europe, or even to India. He took little money with him, but he had introductions to prominent and interesting people in some of the countries he hoped to visit, and he seems to have planned to survive, as many others have done before and since, as a freelance journalist, writing articles and taking photographs.

Although he was undoubtedly drawn to a life of travel, an ambition that was to be gloriously fulfilled when he became revolutionary Cuba's unofficial Foreign Minister in the early 1960s, he also seems to have been motivated by a desire to move away from Argentina. Like many people from the progressive middle classes to which he belonged, Guevara had shallow roots in Argentina's politics and culture (although he retained a lasting addiction to *yerba mate*). He was never a narrow Argentine nationalist, he never expressed any interest in San Martín or the country's other founding fathers, and he was largely unmoved by the populist experiment of Colonel Juan Perón, then drawing to a close. From the start, his political outlook had a Latin American and internationalist focus that was to be further reinforced by his experience of travel.

Guevara was initially drawn to the Andes much as travellers are attracted there today: by the intrinsic fascination of its pre-Colombian civilization, by the people, the ruins, the scenery, and by the culture that is so unutterably different to the modernity of European-style cities like Buenos Aires. Yet the experience of the journey was to lead him towards something entirely different: a greater understanding of the harsh material conditions of the great mass of the people in Latin America, and the corresponding need to do something to improve their lot. In the two years covered by this narrative Guevara dramatically shifts his outlook. He moves from being a detached and cynical observer to becoming a fully fledged revolutionary, seeking a theoretical framework through which to understand the world, and ardent in his desire to take immediate action to change it.

Ever since he had first begun exploring his native country in 1950, Guevara had been accustomed to write irregular diary entries. Later, as he was to do with his campaign diaries in Cuba and the Congo, he would write up his diary jottings into a more considered narrative. This particular journal, covering the years from 1953 to 1956, appears to have been partially rewritten, though the later section about Guatemala and Mexico is largely unrevised. The manuscript was transcribed by his widow, Aleida March, after Guevara's death. His biographer, Jon Lee Anderson, was shown the original transcribed text by Aleida several years before it was published in Havana, and he noted that it was "apparently largely unabridged, except for several sexually graphic passages that she acknowledges having deleted in the interests of preserving the 'propriety' of her late husband's image". This edition of the narrative is complemented by a number of private letters that Guevara wrote during his expedition to his family (mostly to his mother Celia) and to friends (chiefly an old girlfriend and fellow medical student, Berta Tilda Infante).

The two travellers from Buenos Aires crossed the Bolivian frontier at La Quiaca, just a few score miles to the south of the area where Guevara would embark on a guerrilla campaign some thirteen years later, and meet his death in October 1967. They travelled on up to the cold high plateau of the Altiplano, and stayed in La Paz for several weeks, taking the dangerous road down to the tropical Yungas, and visiting one of the recently nationalized wolfram mines. From Bolivia, they moved on to Peru, making the classic scenic journey across Lake Titicaca to Puno, and then taking the Andean train to Cuzco. Guevara had visited the old Inca capital on his earlier journey the year before, and now once again he set off on the magical expedition from Cuzco to the ancient Inca site of Machu-Picchu.

Guevara had a relentless appetite for history and archaeology, and later in his trip he was to visit the ruins of Tazumal in El Salvador and Quiriguá in Guatemala. He made efforts to reach Copán in Honduras, but was refused a visa, and his hopes of seeing the great pyramids at Tikal and Piedras Negras were frustrated by the counter-revolution in Guatemala. Arriving eventually in Mexico, he was able to have his fill of old ruins, making expeditions to Oaxaca and Palenque, as well as to Chichén-Itzá and Uxmaal.

Yet what had begun as an expedition with little aim or purpose developed over time into a *via crucis*, as Guevara became increasingly aware of the political foreground in all the countries that he was moving through. Bolivia had experienced a radical revolution only a year earlier, with peasants and tin miners uniting behind the Movimiento Nacional Revolucionario, led by Víctor Paz Estenssoro, and demanding far-reaching reforms. The old army had initially been disbanded, the three great tin holdings of Patiño, Hochschild and Aramayo had just been nationalized, and a far-reaching land reform programme was announced in August 1953, during Guevara's visit.

Guevara was intrigued by what he saw, but he was far from impressed by the calibre of Bolivia's revolutionary leadership and he was cynical about the commitment of the rank and file. He guessed, rightly, that this was not a revolution that would challenge the hegemony of the United States in Latin America. Writing to his student friend Tita Infante, who had been a member of the Young Communists in the medical faculty of the University of Buenos Aires, he began – amid youthful banter – to make serious political points about the difficulties facing the Bolivian government. While his interest had been aroused in the possibility of revolutionary change, he was clearly disappointed by what he had seen and experienced in Bolivia. He still retained his disdain for Bolivia's 1952 revolution when he returned to the country in 1966 to launch a guerrilla war.

Later on his Andean journey, when he arrived in Ecuador, he fell in with a group of left-wing Argentine exiles, and heard first-hand news of another revolutionary experiment, this time in Central America. His new friends expressed considerable interest and enthusiasm for the revolutionary government of Colonel Alfredo Arbenz in Guatemala, an experience that appeared to be considerably more radical than anything he had witnessed in Bolivia.

Funds permitting, Guatemala was to be his new destination. He dispensed with Calica, his fun-loving but non-political comrade (who set off for Venezuela on his own), and took ship with one of his new acquaintances from the Ecuadorean port of Guayaquil to Panama. From there, he travelled up by land through Costa Rica, El Salvador and Honduras until he reached Guatemala City, then in the final months of a revolutionary process that had enraged the United States. He arrived there on Christmas Eve, 1953. Six months later, in June 1954, he was present when the Arbenz government was overthrown by a military coup, master-minded and supported by the Central Intelligence Agency of the United States.

Guevara's six-month experience in Guatemala was to be the turning-point of his life. He observed at first-hand a radical government, backed by leftist parties, including the Communists, that had embarked on a serious programme of reform. Colonel Arbenz had been elected president in 1950, and had pledged to continue the reformist programme of his predecessor, Juan José Arévalo. Neither Arévalo nor Arbenz was a Communist, or even a socialist, but they expressed a certain nationalistic hostility to United States hegemony in Latin America, partly due to the support given by the Americans to the old Guatemalan dictator, Jorge Ubíco, overthrown in 1944.

In the Cold War atmosphere created by the Korean war, the Americans were openly mistrustful of Colonel Arbenz. His failure to join the American strategic plan for the continent, embodied in the Rio Defence Pact of 1947, had already led the Americans to impose an arms embargo, obliging his government to seek alternative weapons' supplies in Eastern Europe. An ambitious land-reform decree signed in 1952, just a year before a similar reform in Bolivia, proved the final straw for the Americans, for it involved the nationalization of the uncultivated land belonging to the American-owned United Fruit Company, an enterprise in which John Foster Dulles and his brother Allen Dulles, respectively the US Secretary of State and the head of the CIA, were both intimately connected. Plans were put in train by President Eisenhower to organize Arbenz's overthrow.

From Guevara's diary entries, something can be gleaned of the atmosphere in Guatemala City at that time, although much of his efforts were taken up with seeking work and combatting the inevitable bureaucracy that made this such a difficult task. The whole country, mestizos and Indians, seemed to be mobilized behind the government, although in reality this proved to be something of an illusion.

In one sense the Americans were right to be preoccupied by Guatemala, for the country in the early 1950s had become a mecca for leftists from all over Latin America, rather as Cuba was to become in the 1960s, Chile in the 1970s, and Nicaragua in the 1980s. Political discussions lasted all night, with participants from the entire continent telling their own stories, and offering their particular experiences for general illumination. These are rare moments in history, and Guevara was there in the thick of it, enjoying every moment. He had also found a new girlfriend, Hilda Gadea, a revolutionary intellectual from Peru with whom he could hone his argumentative and dialectical skills, someone closer at hand than Tita Infante, his abandoned friend in Buenos Aires.

The CIA coup in June 1954 put an end to Guevara's first introduction to revolutionary euphoria. Along with many other foreign leftists, he took refuge in the Argentine embassy, and was eventually allowed to leave for Mexico. He never forgot his experiences in Guatemala, or the lessons he had learnt. They were to have a direct influence on the radical strategy adopted by the Cuban revolution. Welcoming Arbenz to a conference in Havana six years later, in August 1960, Guevara expressed his gratitude to the former president "and to the democracy that gave way, for the example that they gave us, and for the accurate estimate they enabled us to make of the weaknesses that government was unable to overcome. This allowed us to go to the root of the matter, and to behead those who held power, and their lackeys, at a single stroke."

Once established in Mexico City, Guevara continued the endless task of finding work to make ends meet. But he was no longer a traveller seeking fresh horizons. He had arrived at his penultimate destination, supported by an ever enlarging group of revolutionary comrades. In December 1956, he joined the expeditionary force on board the *Granma* that set sail for Cuba. Meeting Castro in the summer of 1955, he had had no hesitation in linking his own personal future to that of the Cuban revolution. The callow youth who had left Buenos Aires two years earlier, uncertain of his mission or his destination, had finally discovered what he had been looking for.

RICHARD GOTT

Bibliography

Jon Lee Anderson, *Che Guevara, a revolutionary life*, Bantam Press, 1997

Hilda Gadea, *Ernesto: a memoir of Che Guevara*, W H Allen, 1973

Ernesto Guevara, *The Motorcycle Diaries: a journey around South America*, Fourth Estate, London, 1996

Ricardo Rojo, *My Friend Che*, Grove Press, 1969

Ernesto Guevara Lynch, *Aqui va un soldado de América*, Plaza & Janes, Barcelona, 2000

Ernesto Guevara Lynch, *Mi hijo el Che*, Plaza & Janes, Barcelona, 2000

Adys Cupull & Froilan Gonzalez, *Càlida Presencia: la amistad del "Che" y Tita Infante a través de sus cartas*, Editorial Oriente, Santiago de Cuba, 1997

PANAMA CITY
Balboa

COLOMBIA

ECUADOR
Guayaquil
Porto Bolívar
Tumbes

PERU

Lima

Machu Picchu
Cuzco
Lake Titicaca
Puno

BOLIVIA

BRAZIL

Villazón
La Quiaca

ARGENTINA

URUGUAY

Buenos Aires

SCALE
0   500 miles

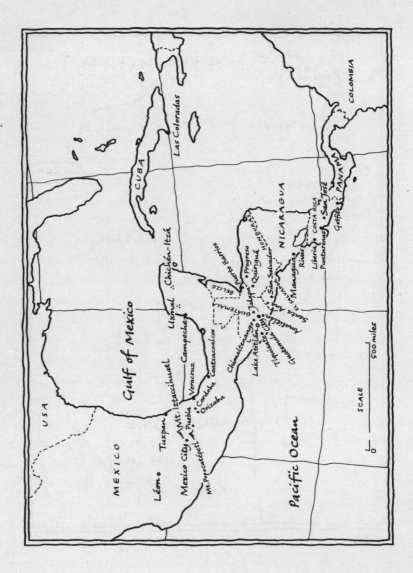

BACK ON THE ROAD

★

The sun shone timidly on our backs as we walked through the bare hills of La Quiaca. I mentally went over the most recent events: my departure, with so many people and a few tears thrown in; the strange looks of the people in second class at the sight of so many fine clothes, leather coats, etc. saying goodbye to a couple of odd-looking snobs loaded down with baggage. My helper's name has changed: Alberto is now called Calica.[1] But the trip is the same: two separate wills moving out through the American continent, not knowing the exact aim of their quest nor in which direction lies their objective.

A grey mist around the bare hills gives a special shade and tone to the countryside. Opposite us a trickling stream separates Argentina from the territory of Bolivia. The two flags face each other across a tiny little railway bridge, the Bolivian new and brightly coloured, the other old, dirty and faded, as if it has begun to understand the poverty of its symbolism.

We get chatting with some policemen who tell us that one of their colleagues is a Cordoban from Alta Gracia, the town of our childhood. He turns out to be Tiqui Vidora, one of the children I used to play with. A strange rediscovery in this northern corner of Argentina.

An unrelenting headache plus my asthma was forcing me to slow down. So we spent three exceptionally boring days in the village there before setting off for La Paz. When we said we were travelling second class, this immediately caused people to lose interest in our journey. But here as elsewhere, they did find it important that a good tip might be forthcoming.

1 He recalls his friend Alberto Granado, who accompanied him on his first trip around Latin America, and refers to Carlos Ferrer (Calica), his companion on this second trip that began on 7 July 1953. (All the notes in this diary are supplied by the Archivo Personal del Che.)

Now we are in Bolivia and on our way, after a superficial inspection by the Argentine and Chilean customs.

From Villazón the train struggles on north through completely dry hills, gorges and tracks. Green is a forbidden colour.

The train's appetite picks up again on the arid plains, where saltpetre begins to put in an appearance. But then night falls and everything is lost in the gradually spreading grip of the cold. We have a cabin now, but in spite of the extra blankets and everything a faint chill enters our bones.

The next morning our boots are frozen and we have an uncomfortable sensation in our feet. The water is iced up in the toilets and even in our carafes.

Dishevelled and with unwashed faces, we feel ill at ease as we make our way to the dining car.

But the faces of our fellow-travellers make us feel much more relaxed.

At 4.00 in the afternoon the train arrives in the La Paz gap. A small but very beautiful city lies scattered about the rugged background terrain, with the perpetually snow-covered figure of Mount Illimani as its sentinel. The last few kilometres take more than an hour to complete. The train seems to be passing by the side of La Paz, when it turns back and continues its descent.

It is Saturday afternoon and the people recommended to us are very difficult to find, so we spend our time changing and removing the grime left from our journey.

On Sunday we start looking for the people recommended to us and making contact with the Argentine community.

La Paz is the Shanghai of the Americas. The widest range of adventurers of all nationalities vegetate and prosper in the midst of a colourful mestiza city that is leading the country to its destiny. The "well-to-do", refined people are shocked at what has been happening and complain bitterly about the new importance conferred on Indians and mestizos, but in all of them

I thought I could detect a spark of nationalist enthusiasm for some of what the government has done.

No one denies that it is necessary to end the state of affairs symbolized by the power of the three tin-mine bosses, and young people think this has been a step forward in the struggle to make people and wealth more equal.

On the evening of 15 July there was a torchlight procession. It was long and boring as a demonstration, but interesting because the way people expressed their support was by firing off a Mauser or a "Piri-pipi", the wonderful repeater rifle.

The next day, guilds, high schools and trade unions marched past in a parade that never seemed to end, making the Mausers sing out rather often. After a certain number of paces, one of the leaders of the quasi-companies into which the parade was divided would always shout out: "Comrades from such and such a union, long live La Paz, long live American independence, long live Bolivia! Glory to the early martyrs for independence, glory to Pedro Domingo Murillo, glory to Guzmán, glory to Villaroel!" The recitation was given in a tired voice, suitably framed by a monotonous choral accompaniment. It was a picturesque but not virile demonstration. The weary gait and the general lack of enthusiasm robbed it of vital energy; what was missing, said those in the know, were the energetic faces of the miners.

Another day we took a lorry to Las Yungas. At the start we climbed up to 4,600 metres at a place called The Summit, then slowly came down a cliff road with a steep drop nearly always to our side. We spent two magnificent days in Las Yungas, although we could have done with two women to add the necessary erotic touch to the greenery surrounding us on all sides. On the lush slopes that fell protected by a cloudy sky down to a river many hundred metres below, there was scattered cultivation of coconut palms with their typically ringed trunks, banana trees looking at a distance like green shoots spiralling out from the forest, orange and other citrus trees, and coffee trees reddened with their fruit. Some variety was introduced by

5

the stunted form of a papaya tree, which is a little reminiscent of the static shape of a llama or of other tropical fruits and trees.

On one patch of land a farm was being used as a school by Salesian priests, one of whom, a German, showed us round with great courtesy. Fruits and vegetables were being carefully grown there in large quantities. We did not see the children (they were at a class), but when he spoke of similar farms in Argentina and Peru I remembered the indignant words of a teacher I once knew: "As a Mexican educationalist said, they are the only place in the world where animals are treated better than people." I did not say anything in reply. But the Indian continues to be an animal for the white mind, especially for Europeans, whichever holy order they belong to.

We did the return journey in the van of some guys who had spent the weekend in the same hotel. We looked rather strange by the time we reached La Paz, but it was quick and fairly comfortable.

La Paz, naive and simple like a girl from the provinces, proudly shows off its wonderful buildings. We visited its new edifices, the pocket university whose terraces tower over the whole city, the municipal library, and so on.

The extraordinary beauty of Mount Illimani spreads its soft glow, with a halo of snow that nature has given it for all eternity. It is in the twilight hours that the solitary peak is at its most solemn and imposing.

There is a man here from an hidalgo family in Tucumán who reminds me of the mountain's august serenity. Exiled from Argentina, he has become the central focus of the Argentine community in La Paz, which looks on him as a leader and a friend. His political ideas have long been antiquated everywhere in the world, but he keeps them apart from the proletarian hurricane that has broken loose on our warring planet. He holds out his friendly hand to any Argentine, without asking who he is or why he has come. And over us poor mortals radiates his august serenity, his patriarchal, everlasting protection.[2]

2 The name of the person in question is Isaías Nogués.

We are left stranded waiting for things to change and become clearer; we shall see what happens on the 2nd. But something sinuous and big-bellied has crossed my path. We shall see . . .

We have at last visited Bolsa Negra. We took the road south up to a height of some 5,000 metres, then descended to the valley at the bottom of which are the mine management and (on one of its slopes) the actual seam.

It is an imposing spectacle. To the back stands Illimani, serene and majestic; to the front, snow-white Mururata; and in front of us, the mine buildings looking like glasses of something that has been thrown from the hillside and remained here at the whim of the irregular terrain. An enormous variety of dark hues shoots the mountain with colour. The silence of the still mine assails even those who, like us, are not familiar with its language.

The reception is cordial; they give us lodging and then we sleep.

The next morning, a Sunday, we went with one of the engineers to a natural lake fed by one of Mururata's glaciers. In the evening we visited the mill where wolfram is obtained from the ore produced in the mine.

In brief, the process is as follows. The rock from the mine is divided into three: one part with a 70 per cent extractable deposit; another part with some wolfram, but in lesser quantity; and a layer containing nothing, which is thrown on to a rubbish heap. The second category goes to the mill on a wire rail or cableway, as they call it in Bolivia; there it is tipped out and sent for pounding into smaller pieces, after which another mill further reduces its size; it is then passed through water several times so that the metal is separated out as a fine dust.

The head of the mill, a very competent man called Señor Tenza, has planned a series of changes that will result in higher output and better exploitation of the mineral.

The next day we visited the gallery. Carrying the waterproof bags we had been given, as well as a carbide lamp and a pair of rubber boots, we entered the dark unsettling atmosphere of the mine. We spent two or three hours checking buffers, seeing seams disappear into the depths of the mountain, climbing through narrow hatches to a different layer, hearing the din of wagon-loads sent down to be picked up at another level, watching the pneumatic drills prepare holes for the load.

But the mine could not be heard throbbing. It lacked the energy of the workers who daily tear their load of materials from the earth, but who were in La Paz defending the Revolution on this 2nd of August, the Day of the Indian and of the Agrarian Reform.

The miners arrived in the evening, stony-faced and wearing coloured plastic helmets that made them look like warriors from other lands.

The spectacle of their impassive faces held our interest as the mountain echoed back the sound of unloading and the valley made the lorry carrying them seem smaller than it was.

Bolsa Negra can go on producing for another five years under present conditions. Then it will come to a standstill unless a gallery several thousand metres long is linked up with the seam. Such a gallery is planned. Nowadays this is the only thing that keeps Bolivia going; it is a mineral that the Americans will buy and the government has ordered production to be stepped up. A 30 per cent increase has been achieved thanks to the intelligence and tenacity of the engineers in charge. Doctor Revilla was very kindly waiting to invite us into his home.

We took advantage of a lorry and set off back at 4.00. Having spent the night in a small town called Palca, we arrived in La Paz early the next day.

Now we are waiting for a [?]³ to be on our way.

Gustavo Torlincheri is a great artist-photographer. In addition to a public exhibition and some pictures in his private collection, we had a chance to see his manner of working. A simple technique, completely subordinate to methodical composition, results in photos of remarkable quality. We

3 Word illegible.

8

went with him on an Andean Club trip from La Paz which took in Chacoltoya and then the water outlets belonging to the electricity company that supplies La Paz.

Another day I went to the Ministry of Peasant Affairs, where they treated me with the utmost courtesy. It is a strange place: masses of Indians from various groups in the Altiplano wait their turn to be given an audience. Each group, dressed in typical costume, has a leader or indoctrinator who speaks to them in their own native language. When they go in, the employees sprinkle them with DDT.

Finally everything was ready for our departure. Each of us had his amorous connection to leave behind. My farewell was at a more intellectual level, without the sweetness, but I think there is something between us – between her and me.

The last evening was one of libations at Nogués's house – so many that I forgot my camera there. Amid great confusion, Calica left alone for Copacabana, while I stayed on another day and used it to sleep and to retrieve my camera.

After a very beautiful trip along the lake, I crossed La Bolsa at Taquería and arrived in Copacabana. We stayed in the best hotel there and hired a boat to take us across the next day to Isla del Sol.

They woke us at 5.00 in the morning and we set off for the island. The wind was very poor, so I had to do some rowing.

We reached the island at 11.00 and visited an Inca site. Later I found out there were other ruins, so we forced the boatman to go to them. It was interesting, especially the scratching around among the ruins. We found some relics there, including an idol representing a woman who nearly fulfilled my dreams. The boatman showed no eagerness to return, but we persuaded him to set sail. He made a complete hash of things, however, and we had to spend the night in a wretched little room with straw for a mattress.

We rowed back the next morning, making hard work of it because of our state of tiredness. We wasted the day sleeping and resting, then made up our minds to leave by mule the next morning. But we thought better of it and decided instead to leave it until the afternoon. I booked us on a lorry, but it left before we arrived with our bags, so we were stuck until we finally managed to get there in a van. Then our odyssey began, as we had to walk two kilometres with our heavy luggage on our backs. We eventually got hold of a couple of porters and, with a lot of laughing and cursing, reached the place where we were due to stay. One of the Indians, whom we called Túpac-Amaru, looked a sorry sight: each time he sat down to rest, he was unable to get up again without our help. We slept like a log.

The next day we were unpleasantly surprised to find that the policeman was not in his office, so we watched the lorries leave without being able to do anything. The day passed in total boredom.

The next day, comfortably installed in a "Couchette", we headed along the lake towards Puno.[4] Near the lake some *tolora* were blossoming, which we had not seen since Taquira. On reaching Puno, I had two of my books confiscated at the last customs post: *El hombre en la Unión Soviética*, and a Ministry of Peasant Affairs publication, which they loudly accused of being "Red, Red, Red". After some banter with the main policeman I agreed to look for a copy of the publication in Lima. We slept in a little hotel near the railway station.

When we were about to climb with all our luggage into our second-class compartment, a secret policeman suggested with an air of intrigue that we go into first class and travel free to Cuzco with the badges belonging to two of them. Of course we agreed to this and had ourselves a comfortable ride, giving the two guys what the second-class tickets would have cost.

4 Ernesto's stay in Bolivia lasted for more than a month, although the exact dates do not appear in his passport. But from a letter to his mother from Cuzco dated 22 August 1953 (reproduced below), we know that he left La Paz on 7 August.

That night, when we reached the station in Cuzco, one of them disappeared, leaving his badge in my possession. We stayed in a little dump of a hotel and had a good night's sleep.

The next day we went to check our passports and met a secret policeman who asked us in the professional sort of way they have where the badge was that I had had the night before. I explained what had happened and handed over the badge. We spent all the rest of the day visiting churches, and the next day as well. We have now seen all the most important things in Cuzco, if a little superficially, and are waiting for an Argentine lady to change some of our money into sols so that we can go to Machu-Picchu and have a look round.

We've got our sols, but only 600 for 1,000 pesos. I don't know how much this was down to the Argentine woman, because the agent did not put in an appearance. Anyway, for the moment we are safe from hunger.

Letter to his mother
Cuzco, 22 [August 1953]

You supply the epigraph, mum.

It has again been a great pleasure for me and I almost feel like a rich man, but the effect is different this time. Alberto has put on a show with talk about marrying Inca princesses and regaining empires. Calica keeps cursing the filth and, whenever he treads on one of the innumerable turds lining the streets, he looks at his dirty shoes instead of at the sky or a cathedral outlined in space. He does not smell the intangible and evocative matter of which Cuzco is made, but only the odour of stew and excrement. It's a question of temperament.

All this apparent incoherence – I'm going, I went, I didn't go, etc. – corresponded to the necessity that they should think us to be outside Bolivia, for a revolt was expected at any moment and we had the earnest intention to stay and see it at close range. To our disappointment it did not happen, and all we saw were displays of strength by a government which, despite everything I am told, seems to be solid enough.

I had half a mind to go and work in a mine, but I was not willing to stay more than one month and as I was offered a minimum of three I didn't stick to the idea.

Later we went to the shores of Lake Titicaca or Copacabana and spent a day on the Isla del Sol, the famous sanctuary of Inca times. In a cemetery there, I fulfilled one of my dearest wishes as an explorer when I came across a statuette of a woman the size of a little finger, though an idol all the same, which was made of the Incas' famous *chompi* alloy.

On reaching the frontier, we had to walk two kilometres without any transport and for one kilometre it fell to me to carry my suitcase filled with books, which felt like a ton of bricks. The two of us plus a couple of labourers were completely flaked out by the time we arrived.

At Puno there was a hell of a row with the customs people, because they confiscated a Bolivian book of mine saying it was "red". There was no way of persuading them that these were scientific publications.

I don't tell you of my future life because I don't know anything about it, not even how things will go in Venezuela. But we have now got the visa through an intermediary [. . .]; as to the immediate future, I can tell you that I haven't changed my mind about the US$10,000, that I may do another trip in Latin America, only this time in a North-South direction with Alberto, and that maybe it will be in a helicopter. Then Europe and then it becomes unclear.

During these days of waiting, we have exhausted the supply of churches and other places of interest in Cuzco. Again I have in my head a motet of altars, large paintings and pulpits.

The pulpit in the Church of San Francisco impressed me by its simplicity and serenity, in contrast to the overelaborate style dominant in nearly all the colonial structures.

Belén has its towers, but the radiant white of the two bell towers here produces a shock in comparison with the dark hues of the old nave.

My little Inca statue, newly named Martha, is genuine and made of *tunyana*, the alloy used by the Incas. One of the museum staff told me so. It's a pity that we find the vessel fragments, which set the tone of that former civilization, are strange to our eyes. We have been eating better since the payment.

Machu-Picchu does not disappoint; I don't know how many times I can go on admiring it. But those grey clouds, those violet and other-coloured peaks against which the grey ruins stand out so clearly, are one of the most wonderful sights I can imagine.

Don Solo received us very well and charged us for only half the costs of our stay. But despite Calica's enthusiasm for this place, I still miss Alberto's company. The way in which our characters were so suited to each other is becoming more obvious to me here in Machu-Picchu.

Back to Cuzco, to have a look round a church and wait for the departure of a lorry. Our hopes crumble one by one, as the days pass and the pesos or sols grow fewer. We had already got just the lorry we needed and the bags were all loaded when a hell of a row broke out over a couple of pounds in weight that we didn't have. We might have come to a deal if we had been willing to compromise a little, but as it was we were left stranded until the next day, Saturday, and our first calculations indicate that it would have been 40 sols more expensive than on the bus.

Here in Cuzco we got to know a spiritualist medium. It was like this. As we were talking with the Argentine woman and Pacheco, the Peruvian engineer, they began to speak about spiritualism. We had to make an effort not to laugh, but we put a serious face on it and the next day they took us to meet him. The guy reported seeing some peculiar lights – in our cases, the green light of sympathy and the light of egoism in Calica, and the dark green of adaptability in me. Then he asked me if I had something in my stomach, because he saw the glow dimming inside me. This left me wondering, as my stomach was in fact grumbling because of the Peruvian peas and the tinned food. A pity I was unable to have a session with the medium.

Cuzco is already a long way behind us. We reached Lima after a seemingly endless three-day journey by bus. From Abacoy the road followed the ever narrower gorges of the River Abancoy for a whole day. We bathed in a little pool that hardly covered us, and the water was so cold that I did not enjoy it.

The journey was becoming interminable. The poultry had soiled the whole area beneath which we were seated, and an unbearable smell of duck created an atmosphere so thick you could have cut it with a knife. After a few punctures that made the journey drag on even longer, we finally reached Lima and slept like a log in a little dump of a hotel.

On the bus we got to know a French explorer whose boat had sunk on the Apurimac. The current had swept away a companion of his who, though he originally described her as a teacher, turned out to have been a student who ran away from her parents' home and did not know the first thing about anything. The guy is going to have a hard time.

I went to visit Dr Pesce and the people from the leprosarium.[5] They all received me most cordially.

Nine days have passed in Lima, but we have not been to see anything extraordinary because of various engagements with friends. We have got fixed up at a university canteen, though, which charges 1.30 a meal. It's a perfect arrangement for us.

5 Leprosorio De Guia. Both Dr Pesce and Zoraida Boluarte had offered him support and friendship during his first trip in Latin America, so he immediately visited them when he returned to Lima.

Zoraida Boluarte invited us round to her place. From there we went to see the famous 3-D at a cinema. It doesn't seem at all revolutionary to me and the films are the same as before. The real fun came later, when we ran into a couple of policemen who turned everything upside down and took us off to the police station. After spending a few hours there, we were released and told to come back the next day – that is, today. We shall see.

The business with the police didn't come to anything. After a mild interrogation and a few apologies, they let us go. The next day they called us back to ask us about a couple who had kidnapped a boy and bore some resemblance to the Roy couple in La Paz.

The days followed each other without our having the chance to do anything new. The only event of any importance was our change of residence, which has enabled us to live completely gratis.

The new house has worked out magnificently. We were invited to a party, and although I couldn't go because of my asthma it was an opportunity for Calica to get sozzled again.

We had one of those nice thorough chats with Dr Pesce in which he speaks with such assurance about such varied subjects.

We can be almost sure about the tickets for Tumbes, which are being arranged by a brother of Señora de Peirano. We are waiting here, with virtually nothing more to see in Lima.

The spineless days keep passing, and our own inertia helps to ensure that we stay in this city longer than we wished. Maybe the question of the tickets will be resolved tomorrow, Monday, so that a final date can be set for our departure. The Pasos have shown up, saying that they have good work prospects here.

We are almost on our way. We have a last few minutes to look at dreamy Lima: its churches may be filled with magnificence inside, but in my view their exteriors do not have the august sobriety of the Cuzco temples. The cathedral has a series of Passion scenes of great artistic value, which give the impression of being by a painter from the Dutch school. But I don't like its nave, or its stylistically amorphous exterior, which looks as it if was built in a period of transition when Spain's martial fury was on the wane and a love of ease and luxury was beginning to take over. San Pedro has a number of valuable paintings, but its interior doesn't please me either.

We bumped into Rojo, who had been through the same tribulations as ourselves but with the additional problem of the books he was carrying. He is heading for Guayaquil and we will meet up there.

By way of farewell to Lima we saw *Gran concierto*, a Russian film dangerously similar to North American ones, but of better quality because of its colour and its musical fidelity. The farewell to the sick was pretty emotional. I'm thinking of writing something about it.

Letter to his friend Tita Infante

Lima, 3 September

Dear Tita,[6]

I'm sorry I must write to you in my beautiful handwriting, but I haven't managed to get a typewriter to cure the problem. Anyway I hope you'll find a free day to spend reading this letter.

Let's get to the point. Thank your friend Ferreira for the letter of introduction to the Bolivian college. Doctor Molina treated me very kindly and seemed to be delighted with me and my travelling companion (whom you met at home). Subsequently he offered me a job as a doctor and Calica a job as a male nurse in a mine; we accepted, but cut to one month the three that he wanted us to stay there. Everything was settled and agreed, and we were supposed to report the next day to finalize the details. How surprised we were the next day when we found out that Dr Molina had left on an inspection of the mines and would only be back in two or three days. We presented ourselves after

6 Berta Gilda (Tita) Infante, a medical student and active member of the Argentine Communist Youth, was very friendly with Ernesto Guevara.

that time had passed and there was no news of Molina, although it was thought that he would return in another couple of days. It would take too long to list the number of times we went looking for him; the fact is that twenty days passed before he came back, and by then we could no longer settle for one month because the time lost would have made it two months, and so he gave us some letters for the man in charge of a wolfram mine and we went to spend two or three days there. It is very interesting, especially as the mine is situated in a magnificent spot. It was altogether a fine trip.

I'll tell you that in La Paz I forgot about my diet and all that nonsense, and that nevertheless I was fine during the month and a half I spent there. We travelled quite a bit out into the surrounding area – for example, to the wonderful tropical valleys of Los Yungas – but one of the most interesting things we did was to study the highly absorbing political panorama. Bolivia is a country that has given a really major example to the American continent. We saw the exact setting of the struggles, the marks left by bullets, and even the remains of a man killed in the revolution and recently discovered in a cornice where the lower part of his body had been blown away by one of those bands of dynamite they wore around the waist. They certainly fought without holding back. Here revolutions are not like in Buenos Aires; two or three thousand dead (no one knows for sure how many) were left on the battlefield.

The fighting still goes on, and almost every night people are wounded by gunfire on one side or the other. But the government is supported by the armed people, so there is no possibility of liquidating an armed movement from outside; it can succumb only as a result of internal dissensions.

The MNR is a conglomerate with three more or less clear tendencies: the Right represented by Siles Suazo, the vice-president and

17

hero of the revolution; the Centre represented by Paz Estenssoro, more slippery but probably as right wing as the first; and the Left represented by Lechín, the visible head of a serious protest movement but personally an upstart much given to partying and chasing women. The power will probably remain in the hands of the Lechín group, who can count on powerful support from the armed miners, but the resistance of other people in the government may prove serious, especially as the army is now going to be reorganized.

Well, I've told you something about the scene in Bolivia. I'll tell you about Peru later, when I've lived here for a while, but in general I think that for Peru Yankee domination has not even meant that fictitious economic prosperity which can be seen in Venezuela, for example.

As to my future life, I know little about where I'll be heading and even less when. We have been thinking of going to Quito and then to Bogotá and Caracas, but we don't know about the way in between. I've recently arrived here in Lima from Cuzco.

I never tire of urging you to visit it if you can, and even more so Machu-Picchu. You won't regret it, I assure you.

I guess that since I left you must have taken at least five subjects, and I imagine you still go fishing for worms in the muck heap. There's not much to be said about vocations, but if one day you change your tune and want to see the world,

remember this friend

who for you would risk his life

to help as best he can

when the moment comes.

A hug. Until it occurs to you – and until I reach where it occurs to you,

Ernesto

The first day got us to Piura without a break; we arrived there at lunch time. I, with my asthma, locked myself into my room and only went out for a short while in the evening to see something of the town. It is like a typical provincial capital in Argentina, though with more new cars.

The next day, having agreed with the driver that we should pay less, we took the bus to Tumbes and arrived there as night was falling. The journey took us through Talara, a rather picturesque oil port.

I didn't get to know Tumbes either, because of my asthma, and we continued our journey to the frontier at Aguas Verdes and crossed over to Huaquillas,[7] not without suffering the assaults of the gangs who do the transporting from one side of the frontier bridge to the other. A wasted day in travelling terms, which Calica used to scrounge a few beers.

The next day we set out for Santa Marta, where a river boat took us as far as Puerto Bolívar. We then did an all-night crossing to Guayaquil and arrived the next morning, I still with my asthma.

There we met Big Rojo, though now he was not alone but with three friends[8] of his who were studying law. They took us to the *pensión* where they were staying; there were six of us in all and we formed a closed student circle with our last rings of *mate*. The consul proved impervious to our attempts to touch him for some leaves.

Guayaquil, like all these ports, is an excuse for a city without a life of its own, revolving around the daily arrival and departure of ships.

I couldn't get to know much, because we were too absorbed by the travellers' tales of the guys leaving for Guatemala, one of them with Big Rojo. I later met a young guy, Maldonado,[9] who put me in touch with

7 They arrived in Ecuador on 27 September 1953 and went through immigration on the 28th.
8 They were the Argentine students Andrews Herrero, Eduardo (Gualo) García and Óscar Valdovinos.
9 Doctor Jorge Maldonado Reinella.

some medical people: Doctor Safadi[10], a psychiatrist and a *bolche*[11], like his friend Maldonado. It was through them that I made contact with another leprosy specialist.

They have a confined colony with thirteen people living in quite precarious conditions, for whom there is little specific treatment.

At least the hospitals are clean and not all that bad.

My favourite pastime is chess, which I play with the people at the *pensión*. My asthma is rather better. We are thinking of staying another couple of days, so that we can try to locate Velasco Ibarra[12] here.

Plans made and unmade, financial worries and Guayaquilian phobias. All this is the result of García's passing joke: "Say, you guys, why don't you go with us to Guatemala?"[13] The idea was lying there somewhere; it only needed that little push for me to make up my mind. Calica followed me. Now come feverish days of hunting. The visas have almost been granted, but for an estimated expenditure of $200 it will be hard to make up $120.80 – although we'll do it by trying to sell our luggage. The trip to Panama is free, except for the $2 a head per day which make a total of $32 for the four of us; that's what the discussion has been about, because it can always be cancelled. Hard days await us in Panama.

The meeting with Velasco Ibarra was a lamentable failure. The master of ceremonies, a Señor Anderson, answered our pathetic requests for assistance by saying that life has its ups and downs, that now we are in a down but some ups will come too, and so on.

On Sunday I got to see some places on the coast that are like a rainy zone liable to river flooding. But it was the company of Dr Fortunato Safadi, and of a friend of his who sells insurance, which made the trip especially interesting. A little further on, he said that hard times await us in Panama – what we need to know is whether Panama itself awaits us. After picking up the

10 Doctor Fortunato Safadi.
11 Like the English "bolshy", a term used to indicate his Communist (Bolshevik) affiliation.
12 Several times elected president of Ecuador.
13 See below the letter to his mother from Guayaquil, dated 21 October 1953.

Guatemalan visa without any difficulty, we tried to go and get the boat tickets without the other visa for Panama, but all hell broke loose because the company representative flatly refused to sell them to us without first wiring the Compañía Colón Panamá. The answer came back the next evening and was a definite "no". That was a Saturday. The *Guayos*, a small boat that had been due to leave on Sunday, has postponed its departure until Wednesday.

Calica set off for Quito in a private lorry, at someone else's expense.

On Monday we tried again – this time with a money transfer for 35 dollars in the name of García and myself – because we were determined to leave first. The result was negative, and with no other card in our hand we sent a telegram to Calica telling him to wait for us. That evening I met Enrique Arbuiza, the insurance salesman, who told us that he might be able to arrange things, and the next morning, today, we met the representative of a tourist company. He also refused, but he gave us a different hope by saying that the company which would take us to Panama could issue us with a ticket. The insurance salesman therefore took me along to see the captain of the *Guayos*, who was a friend of his, and put the problem to him. The captain nearly blew his top, but he calmed down after we had explained a few things to him, and it was agreed that we would receive the final answer this afternoon.

Anyway we sent another telegram to Quito, correcting the previous one and telling Calica to go on alone, at least to Bogotá. Our plan is to wait for the final answer, and then for the two of us to go to Panama, or for the three of us to clear out of here as soon as possible.

We shall see . . .

We haven't seen anything. We spent an hour and a bit waiting in vain for the captain of the *Guayos* to show up. Tomorrow we shall decide once and for all what we do, but in any case Andro Herrero will be staying. He argues that it is necessary for one of us to stay behind as a contact man in Guayaquil, and that it is anyway easier for two to slip through than for three. That's for sure. But we sense something fishy in all this and think that some love affair must be keeping him here; he's so secretive that no one has any idea what he gets up to.

I spent a terrible day laid low with asthma, and with nausea and diarrhoea from a saline purgative. García did nothing all day, so the uncertainty continues.

The visa for Panama is an obsession. When everything was ready, they came up with some stuff that meant forking out 90 sucres more than we had on us right then, so it was put off until this afternoon. But then I met the consul, who invited me to visit an Argentine ship. They treated us pretty well and gave us *mate*, but the consul made me religiously put together the ten sucres for the boat. It is a barge of the type of the *Ana G.*, which holds so many memories for me.[14] I want to make a special note of the following: the soldiers watching over the enrolment offices have the initials "US" on their backs.

We now have the visa with its tremendous words: "Fare paid Panama to Guatemala." There's going to be a fine old row. Today I ate with García on board the Argentine ship, where we were treated like kings. They gave us American cigarettes and we drank wine – not to mention the stew. The rest of the day, zilch.

Two more days: a sad Saturday of uncomfortable farewell, a sad Sunday of further postponement. On Saturday I had the machine all but sold, but at the last moment the residue of my bourgeois desire for property stopped me from doing it; afterwards it was apparently too late, although that will become known only today. The ring could have been placed more or less for sure on Sunday evening. In the morning, when all our plans seemed to be in ruins, without a cent or the possibility of finding any money, the news of the postponement seemed like a gift from heaven. But when the engineer was asked for a date and replied: "Who knows, maybe Thursday", our enthusiasm hit rock bottom. Five more days are another 120 sucres, more difficulty paying for things, etc. etc.

14 The boat on which he enrolled as a medical orderly on his trip round the Caribbean in 1950.

And now more and more days. The machine couldn't be sold, and there's virtually nothing left to burn. So our situation is pretty precarious: not one peso over, debts of 500 and potentially 1,000, but when? that is the question. We'll be leaving now on Sunday, unless there's another delay for some unforeseen reason.

Letter to his mother
Guayaquil [21 October 1953]

I am writing you this letter (who knows when you'll read it) about my new position as a total adventurer. A lot of water has flowed under the bridge since my last epistolary news.

Here is the gist. As we were travelling along – Calica, García (one of our acquisitions) and I – we felt a little homesick for the beloved country. We said how good it must be for the two members of the group who had managed to leave for Panama, and we commented on the tremendous interview with XX., that guardian angel who said to me what I will tell you later. The fact is that García, as if in passing, let out an invitation for us to go with them to Guatemala, and I was in the right kind of mood to take it up. Calica promised to give his answer the next day and it was "yes", so that there were four new candidates for Yankee opprobrium. But then the tribulations began at the consulates, with daily laments for the missing visa to Panama, and after various ups and downs (both factual and psychological) he seemed to change his mind to "no". Your masterly suit, pearl of your dreams, died a heroic death in a second-hand shop, and the same happened to all the unnecessary items in my luggage, which has now shrunk considerably for the benefit (I fondly hope) of the economic stability of our trio.[15]

What this means is that if a captain who is a semi-friend of ours

15 The trio consisted of Gualo García, Andrews Herrero and Ernesto, since Calica had left for Venezuala.

agrees to do the necessary, García and I will be able to travel to Panama, and then the combined efforts of those who reach Guatemala, plus those from Panama, will take in tow the straggler left behind as security for the existing debts. If the captain in question fouls it up, the same two buddies will head towards Colombia, again leaving the security here, and then set off for Guatemala in whatever the Almighty unwarily places within their reach.

Guayaquil, 24 [October]. After much toing and froing and quite a lot of calls, plus a discreet bribe, we have the visa to Panama. We leave tomorrow, Sunday, and will be there on the 29th or 30th. I have written this rapidly at the consulate.

Ernesto

Now I'm at sea reviewing the past few days. The feverish searching for someone to give us something for our saleable equipment. The scornful ring-buyer who finally ate humble pie. The ultimate gesture of our friend Monasterio, who gave us 500 sucres and spoke to the landlady at the *pensión*. The moments of farewell, always cold, always less than you expected, when you find yourself incapable of externalizing a deep feeling.

Now we are in a first-class cabin, which for those who pay would be bad but for us is ideal. Our room-mates are a talkative Paraguayan, who is doing a lightning trip by air around the Americas, and a nice guy from Ecuador – both of them pretty hopeless. García got seasick and, after throwing up, has taken a Benadril and is fast asleep. This evening there's a *mate* session with the engineer.

I learnt of the death of an aunt of mine in Buenos Aires, via a diplomat I knew in Chile and unexpectedly met again on the Argentine ship. He told me the news as if in passing.

Marta, they say, has nothing of value; we didn't get off at the port. But the next day at Esmeraldas we really splashed out and spent a dollar visiting the whole town, as a way of marking our departure from Ecuador.

One of our companions, the Ecuadorian, came across a cousin he had never met before but with whom he became quite friendly. They took us for a stroll on the outskirts of town, among tropical mountains.

Then we had a whole day at sea; I thought it was beautiful, but it did not please Gualo García one little bit. On the way out from Esmeraldas they discovered a tramp – that is, a stowaway – who was returned to port. It brought back pleasant memories from other times.

Now we are settled in Panama,[16] without a clear destination, without anything clear at all except the certainty of leaving. Incredible things have happened. Let's take them in order. We arrived and nothing happened; the customs inspector calmly looked through our things, the other official stamped and returned our passports, and we set off for Panama City from Balboa, our port of disembarkation.

Big Rojo had left the address of a *pensión*, so we went there and they put us in a corridor for a dollar a day each.

Nothing new happened that day, but the big surprise came the day after. On opening our letters at the Argentine consulate, we found one from Rojo and Valdovinos in which they announced the latter's marriage. We found it all most puzzling, until Luzmila Oller[17] came and told us about the wedding and other things. They set off a revolution in the family: the father has done a bunk; the mother won't have him in the house; and the guy just went straight on to Guatemala, without having a screw or even, it seems, a serious bout of passion.

The girl is very nice and seems quite intelligent, but she's too Catholic for my taste.

The Argentine consul may be able to arrange something for us. Perhaps

16 In a letter of 21 October 1953, Ernesto estimates that he will reach Panama between the 29th and the 30th of the month. The departure was on 25 October.
17 The daughter of a Panamanian member of parliament.

we'll write for a magazine called *Siete*, perhaps I'll give a lecture. So we may have something to eat tomorrow.

Nothing new – except that tomorrow I am to give a lecture on allergy mixed together with something about the organization of the Faculty of Medicine in Buenos Aires. I was given quite a warm welcome at the college. I met Don Santiago Pi Suñer, the physiologist, and in another context we met Dr Carlos Guevara Moreno, who struck me as an intelligent demagogue, very knowledgeable about mass psychology but not about the dialectics of history. He is very nice and friendly and treated us with deference. He gives the impression that he knows what he is doing and where he is going, but he won't take a revolution beyond what is strictly necessary to keep the masses content. He is an admirer of Perón. Maybe we will place two articles: one in *Siete*, the other in the Sunday supplement of *Panamá-América*.

Luzmila has received a 16-page letter from Óscar Valdovinos. She is oozing happiness.

I gave the famous lecture to an audience of twelve, including Dr Santiago Pi Suñer, for $25. I wrote a report on Amazonia, $20, and one on Machu-Picchu, probably $25.

We are going to move to a place we'll have for free. We met a young painter, not a bad type. They are half inclined to expel the boys from the FUA because they went to the consulates and travelled in a foundation aeroplane from Guayaquil to Quito, and they've got Valdovinos screwed in Guatemala because he sent a statement on behalf of "some anti-Peronist Argentine youth". I don't know if it will all be sorted out. We went for a very pleasant walk on the beach at Riomar with Mariano Oteiza, president of the Panama Students Federation.

My report on Amazonia has appeared in *Panamá-América*;[18] the other

18 The articles appeared as 'Un vistazo a las márgenes del gigante de los ríos', *Suplemento dominical Panamá-América*, 22 November 1953, p. 10; and 'Machu-Picchu, enigma de piedra en América', *Suplemento semanal Siete*, 12 December 1953, p. 18. For an English translation, see the appendix below.

one is struggling for a place. Our situation is bad. We don't know how we'll be able to leave here. The Costa Rican consul is a useless half-wit and he won't give us a visa. We met a sculptor, Manuel Teijeiro, who is an interesting man.

The struggle is getting heavy. Met the painter Sinclair, who studied in Argentina. A good guy.

Best so far are the trio consisting of Adolfo Benedetti, Rómulo Escobar and Isaías García. All very fine kids.[19]

We still haven't really got to know the Canal. We went there too late the other day and it was closed.

I should add another two names: Everaldo Tómlinson and Rubén Darío Moncada Luna.

The last few days in Panama were a waste of time. The Costa Rican consul didn't want to give us the visas unless we showed him not only a ticket out of the country but also a ticket in. We needed Luzmila to lend us the money. We couldn't get the camera out, nor get the PAA to refund the fare to Costa Rica. We missed a farewell party they gave for Luzmila – or rather, I missed it, because Gualo had a complex about the way they looked at us and didn't want to go anyway. Luzmila behaved a little coldly in the end.

They gave me $15 for the second little piece, thanks to the efforts of another good guy, José María Sánchez.

We left Panama with $5 in our pockets. At the last moment we met an interesting figure from Córdoba, Ricardo Lutri, a botanist and asthmatic who has been in Amazonia and Antarctica and is thinking of doing a trip round Central America and through Paraguay, the Amazon and the Orinoco – my old idea.

Now we are in the centre of Panama; the springs on the lorry that took us are completely broken, and there is no sign of the driver who went to David in search of a replacement. We had an egg and a little rice for

19 All members of the Panama Students Federation.

27

breakfast. By night the mosquitoes don't let you sleep, by day the mosquitoes don't let you live (poetic). It is a fairly high region, not at all hot, with masses of trees and huge downpours.

I paid a lightning visit to Palo Seco. There were a couple of American Jews who have been living there for twenty years; they don't seem very knowledgeable, but they devote themselves wholeheartedly to the sick.

Rubén Darío Moncada got it only half right. The driver turned out to be a hound from hell, and we were laid low when the brakes failed at a bend. I was in the upper part, so when I saw the disaster happening I threw myself as far as possible and rolled a little further until I came to a halt with my head in my hands. When the drama was over, I ran to help the others and realized that nobody else had anything wrong – only I came out of it with a grazed elbow, torn trousers and a very painful right heel.

I slept the night in the house of Rogelio, the lorry driver, while Gualo stayed on the road watching our things.

The next day we missed the 2.00 train and had to resign ourselves to catching the one at 7.00 the following morning. From the end of the line at Progreso we had to "foot it" to the coast in Costa Rica, where we were received very well. In spite of my bad foot I played football.[20]

We left early the next morning, and after losing our way we got on to the right path and walked for two hours through a muddy area. Then we came to the railway terminal, where we got talking with an inspector who, as it happened, had wanted to go to Argentina but had not been given leave. We reached the port and asked the captain to lend us the fare. He agreed, but we were not given any accommodation. Two employees took pity on us, so here we are sleeping on the floor in their room and feeling very happy.

The famous *Pachuca*, so called because it transports *pachucos* (down-and-outs), will leave the port tomorrow, Sunday. We have a bed. The

20 The date of arrival in Costa Rica was 1 December 1953.

hospital is a comfortable house where you can get proper medical attention, but the degree of comfort depends on the grade of the person working in the company.[21] As always, the class spirit of the gringos makes itself felt.

Golfito is a true gulf, with quite deep water, which can easily take ships of 26 feet. It has a little wharf and enough housing to accommodate the ten thousand company employees. It is certainly hot, but the location is very beautiful. Hills a hundred metres high rise almost from the sea shore, their slopes covered with tropical vegetation that surrenders only when man is constantly present on top of it. The town is divided into clearly defined zones, with guards who can prevent anyone from moving across, and of course the best zone is that of the gringos. It looks a little like Miami, but naturally the poor are not in the same place and are shut up in the four walls of their own homes and in the narrow group to which they belong. Food is the responsibility of a good guy who is now also a good friend: Alfredo Fallas.

Medina is my room-mate and also a good guy. There is a Costa Rican student of medicine, a doctor's son, as well as a Nicaraguan teacher and journalist in voluntary exile from Somoza.

The *Pachuca* left Golfito at one in the afternoon, with us on board. We took a lot of food with us for the two-day voyage. In the afternoon the sea became a little rough: the *Rio Grande*, which is the ship's real name, began to fly around. Nearly all the passengers, including Gualo, started vomiting. I stayed outside with a negress who had picked me up – Socorro, as horny as a toad, with 16 years spent on her back.

Quepos is another banana port. It has now been pretty well abandoned by the company, which had to replace the banana plantations with cocoa and palm-oil trees that produce fewer dividends. It has a very fine beach.

I spent the whole day caught between the dodges and smirks of the black woman, arriving in Puntarenas at 6.00 in the evening. We had to wait a

21 The reference is to the United Fruit Company.

29

little because six prisoners had escaped and could not be found. We went to an address given us by Alfredo Fallas, with a letter from him to a Señor Juan Calderón Gómez.

The guy behaved wonderfully well and gave us 21 colones. As we reached San José, we remembered the scornful judgement of a charlatan back in Buenos Aires: "Central America is farms: you've got the Costa Rica farm, the Tacho Somoza farm, and so on."

A letter from Alberto, with luxury trips in his imagination, has made me want to see him again. His plan is to go to the United States in March.

Here we've started firing off blanks in the air. They give us *mate* at the embassy. The friends we had noted down seem no bloody use: one is director and speaker at the radio, a hopeless character. Tomorrow we'll try to see Ulate.

A day half wasted. Ulate couldn't attend to us as he was very busy. Rómulo Betancourt is away in the country. The day after tomorrow we'll appear in the Costa Rica daily paper with photos and everything and a string of huge fibs. We haven't managed to see anyone important, but we did meet a Puerto Rican, a former suitor of Luzmila Oller, who introduced us to some other people. Tomorrow I may visit the Costa Rican leprosarium.

I didn't see the leprosarium, but I did get to meet two excellent people: Dr Arturo Romero, a man of vast culture who has been removed from the board of the leprosarium as a result of various intrigues; and Dr Alfonso Trejos, a research worker and a very fine person. I visited the hospital, and just this morning the leprosarium. We have a great day ahead, chatting with a Dominican short-story writer and revolutionary, Juan Bosch, and with the Costa Rican Communist leader Manuel Mora Valverde.

The meeting with Juan Bosch was very interesting. He is a literary man with clear ideas and left-wing tendencies. We didn't speak about literature – just about politics. He described Batista as a thug surrounded by thugs. He is a personal friend of Rómulo Betancourt and spoke warmly in his support, as he did for Prío Socarrás and Pepe Figueres. He says that Perón does not have popular influence in the countries of America, and that in '45 he wrote an article denouncing him as the most dangerous demagogue in the Americas. The discussion went on in a way that was generally very friendly.

In the afternoon we met Manuel Mora Valverde. He is a quiet man, indeed slow and deliberate, but he has a number of gestures which indicate a great inner unease, a dynamism held in check by method. He gave us a thorough account of recent Costa Rican politics:

"Calderón Guardia is a rich man who came to power with the support of United Fruit and local landowners. He ruled for two years until the Second World War, when Costa Rica sided with the Allied powers. The first measure taken by the State Department was to demand the confiscation of land in the hands of German owners, especially if coffee was grown on it. This was done, and the subsequent selling of the land led to obscure deals involving some of Calderón Guardia's team of ministers – deals which lost him the support of all the country's landowners, but not of United Fruit. Those who work for the company are anti-Yankee, as a reaction against its exploitation. In any event, Calderón Guardia was left without any support whatsoever, so that it was even impossible for him to go out into the street because of the boos and whistling directed at him. At that moment the Communist Party offered him its support, on condition that he adopted some basic labour legislation and appointed a new cabinet. Meanwhile Otilio Ulate, then a man of the left, warned his personal friend Mora of a plan to trap him that had been cooked up by Calderón Guardia. Mora went ahead with the alliance, and the Calderón government bathed in popularity as the basic working-class gains began to appear.

"The problem of the succession was then posed, as Calderón's period of office was coming to an end. The Communists, who were in favour of a united front of national reconciliation to pursue the working-class policies of the government, put forward the name of Ulate. The rival candidate,

León Cortés, was totally opposed to this and continued to stand. About that time Ulate, using his paper *El Diario de Costa Rica*, began a vigorous campaign against the labour legislation, so that the left broke apart in the wake of Don Otilio's turn.

"The elections resulted in victory for Teodoro Picado, a faint-hearted intellectual ruined by whisky, who nevertheless had quite left-wing tendencies and formed a government with Communist backing. These tendencies persisted for the whole life of his government, although the chief of police was a Cuban colonel and FBI agent imposed by the United States.

"In its closing stages, the disgruntled capitalists organized a huge strike in banking and industry which the government did not know how to break. The students took to the streets, and some were shot and wounded. Teodoro Picado was seized with panic. The elections were approaching and there were two candidates: Calderón Guardia once more, and Otilio Ulate. Teodoro Picado, in opposition to the Communist view of what should be done, handed over the election machine to Ulate and kept the police for himself. The elections were fraudulent, resulting in a triumph for Ulate. An appeal was then lodged with the electoral commission to declare the result null and void, and the opposition also asked for a ruling about the alleged violations, stating that it would abide by the verdict whatever it might be. The court did not agree to hear the accusation (with one of the three judges dissenting), and so application was made to the Chamber of Deputies and the election result was set aside. The great dispute then took place, with the people by now roused to fever pitch. But here a parenthesis should be introduced.

"In Guatemala, the Arévalo presidency had led to the formation of what came to be known as the Socialist Republics of the Caribbean. In this the Guatemalan president had the support of Prío Socarrás, Rómulo Betancourt, Juan Rodríguez, a Dominican millionaire, Chamorro and others. The original revolutionary plan was to land in Nicaragua and remove Somoza from power, since El Salvador and Honduras would fall without much of a fight.

But Argüello, a friend of Figueres, raised the problem of Costa Rica and its convulsive internal situation, whereupon Figueres flew up to Guatemala. The alliance came into operation; Figueres raised a revolt in Cartago and swiftly took armed control of the aerodrome there, which was necessary for any support to be brought in by air.

"Resistance soon took shape, however, and the people attacked the barracks to obtain weapons that the government was refusing to give them. Being without popular support (Ulate had not joined in), the revolution was doomed to failure. Yet it was the popular forces headed by the Communist Party which carried the day – a conclusion extremely unsettling for the bourgeoisie and Teodoro Picado. In fact, Picado flew to Nicaragua to ask Somoza for weapons, only to run into the problem that a high North American official was present at their meeting. This official demanded, as the price for assistance, that Picado should eradicate Communism in Costa Rica, thereby guaranteeing the fall of Manuel Mora, and that each gun should be sent with a man attached to it (which meant an invasion of Costa Rica).

"Picado did not accept these demands because it would have meant betraying the Communists who had supported him throughout. But the revolution was in its last throes, and the power of the Communists so frightened the reactionary elements in the government that they boycotted the defence until the invaders were at the gates of San José and then abandoned the capital for Liberia, close to Nicaragua. At the same time, the rest of the army went over to the Nicaraguans with all the ammunition at its disposal. Then a pact was made with Figueres, underwritten by the Mexican Embassy, and the popular forces actually laid down their weapons in front of the embassy building. Figueres did not keep his side of the agreement, however, and the Mexican Embassy was unable to enforce it because of the hostility of the US State Department. Mora was deported and it was only by chance that he escaped with his life when the plane in which he was travelling came under machine-gun fire. The plane landed in the US Canal Zone, where the Yankee police arrested him and handed him over to the Panamanian chief of police (at that time Colonel Remón). The Yankee journalists who wanted to question him were expelled, and then he had an altercation with Remón and was locked up. Finally he went to Cuba, from where Grau San Martín expelled him to Mexico. He was able to return to Costa Rica during the Ulate period.

"Figueres faced the problem that his forces consisted of only a hundred Puerto Ricans and the six hundred or so men of the Caribbean Legion. Although he initially told Mora that his programme was designed for a twelve-year period and that he had no intention of surrendering power to the corrupt bourgeoisie represented by Ulate, he had to make a deal with the bourgeoisie and agreed to give up power after only a year and a half – an undertaking he fulfilled after he had fixed the election machinery to his liking and organized a cruel repression. When the time was up, Ulate returned to power and kept it for the appointed four years. It was not a mark of his government to uphold the established freedoms or to respect the progressive legislation achieved under the previous governments; it did, however, repeal the anti-landowner "law on parasites".

"The fraudulent elections gave Figueres victory over the candidate representing the tradition of Calderón, who now lives as a closely watched exile in Mexico. In Mora's view, Figueres has a number of good ideas, but because they lack any scientific basis he keeps going astray. He divides the United States into two: the State Department (very just) and the capitalist trusts (the dangerous octopuses). What will happen when Figueres sees the light and stops having any illusion about the goodness of the United States? Will he fight or give up? That is the dilemma. We shall see."

A day that left no trace: boredom, reading, insipid jokes. Roy, a little old pensioner from Panama, came in for me to look at him because he felt he was dying from a tapeworm. He has chronic salteritis.

The meeting with Rómulo Betancourt was not like the history lesson we got from Mora. He strikes me as a politician with some firm social ideas in his head, but otherwise capable of swaying and bending for what promises the greatest advantage. In principle, he is solidly on the side of the United States. He gave a false idea of the Rio Pact and spent most of the time raging about the Communists.

We said our goodbyes to everyone – especially to León Bosch, who is really a first-rate guy – then took a bus to Alajuela and started hitching. After various adventures we arrived this evening in Liberia, capital of Guanacaste province, which is a windy town of ill repute like those in Santiago del Estero back home.[22]

A jeep took us as far as the road allowed it, and from there we started a long walk beneath quite a strong sun. After more than ten kilometres, another jeep picked us up and took us as far as the little town of La Cruz, where we were invited to have lunch. At 2.00 in the afternoon we set off to do another 22 kilometres, but by 5.00 or 6.00 it was getting dark and one of my feet was hurting badly. We slept in a kind of trough used for storing rice and fought all night over the blanket.

The next day, after walking until 3.00 in the afternoon and making a dozen or so detours round a river, we finally reach Peñas Blancas. We had to stay there because there was no longer anything going to the neighbouring town of Rivas.[23]

The next day turned out to be rainy, but as there was no sign of a lorry by 10.00 we decided to brave the drizzle and set off anyway for Rivas. At that moment Big Rojo appeared in a car with Boston University licence plates. They were trying to get to Costa Rica, but that was impossible because the muddy track on which we got bogged down now and again was the Panama-

22 See in the appendix below: 'Experimento extraordinario es el que se realiza en Bolivia', published in *El Diario de Costa Rica*, 11 December 1953.
23 This is the point at which he went on to Nicaragua, on 22 December.

Costa Rica highway. Rojo was accompanied by the brothers Domingo and Walter Beberaggi Allende. We went on to Rivas and there, close to the town, we ordered a roast with *mate* and *cañita*, a kind of Nicaraguan gin. It was a little corner of Argentina transferred to the "Tacho farm". They went on to San Juan del Sur intending to take the car across to Puntarenas, while we took the bus to Managua.

We arrived in the evening, and I began the round of *pensiones* and hotels to find the cheapest one. In the end we settled on one where for four cordobas we each had a tiny room without electricity.

The next day we tramped round the consulates and encountered the usual idiocies. At the Honduran consulate we ran into Rojo and his friends, who had been unable to get across and were now having second thoughts because of the fantastic price that was charged. Everything was now decided very quickly. We two would go with Domingo, the younger of the Beberaggi, to sell the car in Guatemala, while Big Rojo and Walter would go by plane to San José in Costa Rica.

That evening we had a long session at which each of us said what he thought about the Argentine problem. Rojo, Gualo and Domingo were intransigent radicals, Walter pro-Labour, and myself an independent – or at least that was how Big Rojo saw it. What was most interesting for me was that Walter gave me an idea of the Labour Party and Cipriano Reyes that was very different from the one I had had before. He told us of Cipriano's origins as a union leader, his gradual gaining of prestige among the Berisa meat-packing workers, and his attitude to the Unión Democrática coalition, when he supported the Labour Party (founded by Perón at that time) in the full knowledge of what it was doing.

After the elections, Perón ordered the unification of the party and thereby brought about its dissolution. Then a violent debate began in the Chamber, and the Labourites headed by Cipriano Reyes showed no signs of giving up easily. Finally talks got under way for a revolutionary coup d'état headed by the military under Brigadier de la Collina and his assistant Veles (who betrayed him by going off to tell Perón).

The three main leaders of the Party – Reyes, Beberaggi and García Velloso – were imprisoned and tortured, the first in a barbaric manner. After a time, Judge Palma Beltrán ordered the conditional release of the prisoners into police custody, while the state prosecutor appealed against the sentence. Beberaggi managed to escape when the Chamber was in session and to make his way secretly to Uruguay; all the others were arrested and are still in prison. Walter went to the USA, graduated and became a professor of economics. In a series of radio talks he pulled no punches in characterizing the Perón regime, and he was stripped of his Argentine citizenship.

The next morning, having left the others on the plane, we headed north and reached the border just as it was about to close. All we had was $20. On the Honduran side we had to pay up. Then we crossed the whole of the narrow strip that is Honduras at that point and arrived at the other frontier, but we could not pay because it turned out to be too expensive. We slept out in the open – they on rubber mattresses, I in a sleeping bag.

We were the first to cross the frontier and continued to head north. We made slow progress because a lot of punctures had left us with some lousy spare tyres. We reached San Salvador and set about wangling our visas for free – which proved possible with the help of the Argentine embassy.

Then we went on to the frontier,[24] where we paid the surcharge with a few pounds of coffee. On the other side it cost us a torch. But although we had only $3 in our pockets, we were on our way. Domingo was feeling drowsy and so we stopped to sleep in the car.

After some minor incidents, we reached the *pensión* where Óscar and Luzmila were staying in time for breakfast, but they had half fallen

24 They arrived in Guatemala between 23 and 24 December 1953.

out with the landlady and so we had to find ourselves another *pensión* where we would not have to pay in advance. On the evening of 24 December we went to celebrate at the house of Juan Rothe, an agronomist married to an Argentine woman, and he welcomed us as cordially as if we had been old friends. I slept a lot, drank too much – and was very soon feeling ill.

I spent the following days with an infuriating attack of asthma, laid up both because of that and because of the festivities. I was all right again by the 31st, but I kept strictly to a diet during those celebrations.

I haven't met a single interesting person with whom to have a conversation. One evening I had a long chat with [Ricardo] Temoche, a former APRA deputy. If you listen to him, the only enemy of the APRA is the Communist Party: there's no imperialism and no oligarchy of any significance; the bolshies are the irreconcilable enemy. An economist of the stature of Carlos Dáscoli was at the same event, but I could not speak with him because he was too drunk. After my attack, and at the end of the festivities, we witnessed the end of what had seemed to be a serious romance between Domingo Beberaggi and a girl called Julia. On Sunday he sold the car and flew to Costa Rica.

Juan Rothe, who is going to Honduras as a technician, gave a farewell barbecue before his departure. The only one not tipsy was myself, as I was on a diet. I visited Peñalver,[25] a supporter of Acción Democrática, who has put himself out a bit to arrange something for me. Now I am close to the minister, but he doesn't cut much ice.

At another department I met a strange gringo who writes stuff about Marxism and has it translated into Spanish. The go-between is Hilda Gadea,[26] while Luzmila and I do the donkey work. So far we've made $25. I am giving English-Spanish lessons to the gringo.

25 A Venezuelan exile with whom he later had connections in Mexico.
26 An APRA exile who later became Che's first wife. The *gringo* is Professor Harold White; after the revolution in Cuba he was invited there by "Che" and stayed until his death in 1968.

Another find has been the Valerini couple. She is very pretty, he very given to drink – although he's a good guy. They agreed to introduce us to an *éminence grise* within the government: Mario Sosa Navarro. We'll see what comes of it.

The days pass without anything being resolved. In the afternoon I work a little with Peñalver, but he doesn't pay me anything. In the morning I try to sell paintings of Aesculapius, my idol, who is adored by people here, but that doesn't earn me anything either as no sales are made. Among the interesting people I have met is Alfonso Vanergais, a well-intentioned lawyer and president of the Banco Agrario. Edelberto Torres is a young Communist student and son of Professor Torres,[27] who wrote a life of Rubén Darío. He seems a good guy. Nothing more about the *éminence grise*. I had an intense discussion about political issues with Big Rojo and Gualo, in the house of an engineer called Méndez.

Nothing new about the possibility of finding work. The administrative efforts at the Ministry of Public Health have been unsuccessful. For now the only thing that looks promising is a radio contract, although we haven't got anything out of it yet. We haven't met anyone interesting these last few days. I put on the ACTH from 8.00 until 2.00 and a bit in the afternoon. I'm fine.

No prospects for the near future. The *éminence grise* did not keep the appointment we made with him.

A Saturday without troubles and without glory. The only good thing was a serious chat with Señora Helena de Holst,[28] who is close on many points to the Communists and struck me as a very fine person. In the evening a talk with Mujica[29] and Hilda, and a little adventure with a plumpish schoolteacher. From now on, I'll try to keep the diary every day and get a little closer to the political reality of Guatemala.

A quiet Sunday, until I was asked in the evening to attend one of the

27 The prestigious Nicaraguan intellectual Edelberto Torres Rivas.
28 A Honduran exile.
29 The exiled APRA leader Nicanor Mujica Álvarez.

Cubans who was complaining of bad abdominal pains.[30] I called an ambulance and we waited in the hospital until 2.00, when the doctor decided it was necessary to wait before operating and we left him under observation.

Before that, at a party at Myrna Torres's, I met a girl who showed me some attention and offered the possibility of a job for 40 quetzals. We shall see.

Another day with neither troubles nor glory. There's the prospect of ten quetzals (we'd get $25 commission) plus accommodation. We shall see. The Cuban, at his department, was going to look into it.

Another day with neither troubles nor glory. A refrain that looks alarmingly as if it will repeat itself. Gualo vanished all day and did nothing, and I profited from this to do nothing either. In the evening I went to visit the college where I may be working.

Nothing new happened. I talked to the Bolivian ambassador, a good man and a little more than good in his politics. In the evening we went to the opening of the Second Congress of the CGTG,[31] a confused affair apart from the fine speech made by the delegate from the World Federation of Trade Unions.

Another one gone . . . Evidence has now been published that the plot of which people spoke really did exist. We have the possibility of an order, but it will be necessary to present a programme like respectable people. I am a representative for leather and illuminated hoardings – no job. Plenty of *mate*.

Another day with neither troubles nor glory. There is nothing to be expected from Díaz Rozzoto.[32] I went out with a girl who promises something good. Anita asked us to pay at the *pensión* and Hilda cannot give us more than $10. We owe $60 or more. Tomorrow is Sunday, so we mustn't lose heart.

30 This is the first mention in the diary of the Cubans who mounted the attack on the Moncada and were then in Guatemala. He had contact with them through Myrna Torres, the daughter of Edelberto Torres and a friend of Hilda Gadea.
31 The Confederación General de Trabajadores de Guatemala, the Guatemalan trade union federation.
32 Jaime Díaz Rozzoto, private secretary at the president's office.

Two more days without anything important to change our routine. I've still got my asthma, but it looks as if I'll get it under control. Gualo is off to Mexico with Big Rojo for a month. I have a letter for the director of the IGSS,[33] Alfonso Solórzano; we'll see what happens. If nothing comes of it, one of these days I'll pack my bags and maybe emigrate to Mexico. I have written an article with the grandiose title 'El dilema de Guatemala';[34] it's not for publication, just for my own pleasure. [. . .].[35]

As for the asthma, it is getting worse all the time. I have started drinking *mate* and left off the corn pancakes, but I am still getting worse. Tomorrow I think I'll pull a tooth out and see if that isn't the cause of it all. I'll also see if I can finally solve the currency problem.

More days to add to the diary. Full of inner life and nothing more. A collection of failures of every kind, and unchanging sources of hope. Decidedly I am one given to optimistic fatalism. I have spent these days with asthma, the last few almost totally confined to my room, although yesterday (Sunday) I went to Amatitlán with the Venezuelans and Nicanor Mujica. There was a heated discussion in which they all sided against me, except for Big Rojo, who claims that I don't have the moral qualities to discuss anything. Yesterday I went to see about a possible job as a doctor for 80 a month for an hour's work. At the IGSS they gave me a complete assurance that there is no need to worry. Solórzano was friendly and succinct. Now the day can end with the old full stop. We shall see.

But we haven't seen anything. As I did not feel up to moving, I sent for Gualo to deliver my diploma to them, but then Herbert Zeissig started asking for more particulars about me, whether I was a member of the Party, etc. Hilda did not speak to Señora Helena de Holst but . . . sent her a telegram. The asthma is continuing. Gualo is getting in a bad mood about leaving.

33 The Guatemalan Social Security Institute.
34 For an English translation, see Appendix Three below.
35 The square brackets with dots, here as elsewhere, are a purely personal expression.

Two more days added to the series with nothing new. I didn't move because of the asthma, although it would seem to be approaching a night-time climax with vomiting. Helena de Holst has tried to communicate with me, so in fact that's where I hope for most. Hilda Gadea keeps worrying a lot about me, coming to see me and bringing things. Julia Mejías got me somewhere to stay in Amatitlán for the weekend. Herbert Zeissig dodged a final decision and sent me to see V. M. Gutiérrez to obtain the support of the Communist Party – which seems very unlikely to come.

Yet another day, although hope is returning as my health begins to improve. Today we are finally on the brink and Gualo will definitely leave tomorrow at dawn; he is not sleeping here. Rojo paid half the bill at the *pensión*. I owe 45 quetzals. I still don't know if I'll be going to Amatitlán tomorrow. When Gualo comes I'll know for sure one way or another.

I visited Señora de Holst, who has been very kind in looking after me, but her promises, though doubtless sincere, depend on what the public health minister has to say – and he has already sent me packing. In the evening I called round to see Julia Valerini, who had lost a little boy and had had a terrible headache all day.

Two long days filled with a strange cold, especially in the evenings spent out in the open, with trembling and whatever. After a youth festival organized by Myrna, to which I went with Hilda for a change, I cleared off to the lakeside to sleep and then came the bit with the trembling, etc. The next day, Sunday, I bought some food at the market and walked very slowly to the other side of the lake: I had a wonderful siesta in a quiet spot there, then tried to drink some *mate* but the water was too bitter. After dark I made a fire for a barbecue, but the wood was bad, I was already cold and the barbecue was rubbish. I threw half of it in the lake so that no trace would remain of the abysmal failure.

I was walking back slowly when I met a drunk who made the journey seem shorter. Then a van picked us up and here I am.

Monday had nothing of note, except for Peñalver's report that he was working on a medical job for me. Señora de Holst doesn't know anyone in the PAR, the main party in that department, well enough to ask them for something like that. We shall see.

A day of conscious desperation – that is, based not on cyclical crisis but on a cold analysis of reality. My job as overseer at the Argentine's is the only definite possibility. I've given up the idea of being a doctor at the trade unions; the job in a peasant community and the other one from Helena de Holst are still up in the air. I met Pellecer[36] – he struck me as neither fish nor fowl.

The rest continues on its daily course. I meet people on both the right and the left. If it goes on like this, I'll take the job as billsticker for a while to pay my expenses and other things on top.

I've finally got a letter from home and know what I can expect with the *mate* – it's no. The day passed very easily because I felt listless and stayed in my room drowsing. Boss Dícono didn't leave, only his wife; she gave me a mango that was fit to be thrown away.

Maybe tomorrow I'll go to the country for the job at the settlement.

Several days have passed, two of them at the settlement at La Viña. It's a splendid place, with a landscape like the high mountains in Córdoba and human material to be worked into shape. But the key thing is missing: any wish to pay for a doctor of their own. Everything was fine, but on the way back I realized that something had disagreed with me; my stomach was so bad that I had to vomit everything up, then it calmed down a little. We spent the next day in the small town of Chimaltenango, where the youth festival was being held. It was a very beautiful place and everyone did what they felt like doing; we made up our usual little group with Hilda Gadea, the gringo and a Honduran woman. [. . .]

Monday was nothing special, just another day closer to the finishing line: 1 May.

36 Carlos Manuel Pellecer, peasant leader with Communist affiliations.

After a mix-up over introductions, I went to the farm with Peñalver and he rather demagogically put me forward for the job. The director asked me how much I wanted, and I kept it low at 100 quetzals for twice a week, provided they spend 25 a month on laboratory instruments. I'm due to go there again on Saturday to see what's come of it.

The business at the farm is very murky. Answer postponed. I went to Tiquisate and it didn't go well, but there's some hope of a lesser job, with board and lodging. That just leaves Señora de Holst's one, and the thing with the Argentine. We'll see tomorrow.

It's not tomorrow but the day after, and of course we haven't seen anything. Nor does it look as if we'll be seeing anything in the near future. With my mind completely made up, I tried to see Guerrero but couldn't track him down. The only thing worth mentioning is a letter from Mama telling me that Sara has had an operation and is in quite a bad way; they found cancer in her large intestine.[37]

Today has brought me great happiness, though. Julia Mejías introduced me to García Granados, who said he would give me a job to go to Petén for $125. Authorization still has to come from the union, and I'll try to get this tomorrow. It will be great if it comes off. Tomorrow could be a day of further disappointment or it could be my big day in Guatemala.

I am optimistic.

No longer so optimistic – far from it. I spoke with Sibaja, but he didn't seem to be paying attention. Tomorrow at 4.00 he'll tell me once and for all whether or not he has influenced the union leader; also tomorrow Lily will speak to her brother. Probably it will come to nothing again. We shall see. The work in Geography is continuing, although today I wandered around not doing much.

Two more days, with a bit of hope today. Nothing happened yesterday. Sibaja is completely useless, but today I went on my own account to see

37 Sara de la Sierna, sister of Ernesto's mother.

the union leader. A man eager to keep his job, anti-Communist, given to intrigue, but apparently disposed to help me. I was not sufficiently circumspect, but nor did I risk a lot. He'll give me a final answer on Wednesday.

Two more days added to the concert of complaints, but with a couple of positive results. Yesterday I went to see the former house of Lily's famous brother, very wealthy but with a good consulting room and something of a laboratory. The woman is Italian, and she made me keener to travel in Europe. They have something that you don't find in Indo-Americans. I had a touch of asthma that looked like getting worse, but I gobbled down a few of Ross's pills and it stopped. Today's positive side was the arrival of a kilo of *mate*, as well as a letter from Alberto and Calica mentioning some dough that set me dreaming for a while. Hilda's book is still coming along, though rather slowly. Tomorrow I'll see about going to Sanidad to do some study of parasitic diseases.

Two more days in which nothing seems to have happened. The business of going to El Petén does seem to have been finally resolved, though. [. . .]

El Petén confronts me head on with the problem of my asthma, and I think that is what I need. I have to win without any expedients and I think I'll do it, but it also seems to me that the victory will be due more to my natural qualities – which are greater than my subconscious believes – than to the faith I place in victory. I felt very small when I heard the Cubans making grand assertions with total calmness. I can make a speech ten times more objective and without banalities; I can do it better and I can convince the public that I am saying something true. But I don't convince myself, whereas the Cubans do. Nico[38] left his heart and soul in the microphone and for that reason fired even a sceptic like myself with enthusiasm.

Three days now without anything new, except for an attack of asthma which has me shut up in my rooms. It is Sunday and Hilda has been to the port; I didn't feel up to it. There is nothing definite about the job, although

38 Antonio (Nico) López, one of the group that attacked the Moncada, was on board the *Granma* and died in the struggle.

I guess the final result will be yes. I wish it would be sorted out one way or another so that I can see more precisely how things stand. Financially, the months in the forest will do no more than leave me without debts and with a camera. I'll write to Alberto that the future is unclear as far as the country is concerned. My asthma seems to have relented a bit.

If I'm not much better by tomorrow, I won't move from here. The work business is not resolved, but in principle it seems that it will be sorted out. There will be another communication in a couple of days, and this time it may be final. We shall see.

Two more days in the sun; both little and much has happened. The job is still up in the air, but I have the impression it is mine. I spoke to the union leader, who said he would submit a list of things to ask the contractor.

Two more days without a final resolution of anything. I can say that I'll go to El Petén, although I don't have the slightest assurance that it will happen. I'm half inclined to make a list of necessities. I'm burning to go. Maybe everything will be settled by Monday. Tomorrow Myrna is off on an adventure to Canada.

Myrna has gone, leaving behind a cluster of broken hearts and not knowing which one she herself loves. But the serious thing is that I don't know if I'm going to leave here. Still the same uncertainty . . .

Bad news again. It's a real shaggy dog story. That son of a bitch Andrade would not even receive me; this morning he made me wonder a couple of times what I wanted. I'm left hanging. I don't know what to do.

Two more days without anything happening. My original decision to write straight away to Dr Aguilar has not had any effect;[39] I'll do it only if their answer to me today is "no" or is again evasive. García Granados was also cool. Only Julia answers me.

Work – nothing doing. I still have Dr Aguilar's letter in my pocket. In a while I'll try to see that son of a bitch Andrade and get him to tell me

39 Dr Juan Ángel Núñez Aguilar, a Honduran agronomist and economist, who at the time was president of the Instituto de Fomento de la Producción de Guatemala (INFOP).

something. I guess it's no. I've stopped all my correspondence because of this.

Enthusiasm depends on health and circumstances; both have been letting me down. The job in El Petén looks more and more remote. The letter has already gone to Dr Aguilar, but of course I haven't received an answer. Things are getting really difficult. I don't know what the hell to do. I feel like buggering off – maybe to Venezuela.

More days juicy with promises, if not with results. From Tiquisate, no news. From Buenos Aires, news that Aunt Sara has died. From El Petén, I've stopped counting. From the *pensión*, that I should pay up. From the gringo, that he doesn't like the food at the new *pensión*, and that if it doesn't improve I should swap with him. From Señora de Holst, that I should go and live in her house. That's a summary of what has been happening recently. I'm putting in some practice at the health laboratory in case they summon me to Tiquisate – otherwise I'm just waiting to see what happens. I've promised to pay the *pensión* for at least a month by Saturday, which is just a few days away, but I don't know how I'll stump it up.

Several days have passed and a number of things have happened; they're not very important for the future, but they certainly are for today. Things turned ugly at the *pensión* when I couldn't cough up even five cents on Saturday. I left my watch and a gold chain as security. After pawning my jewellery, I set off for Tiquisate and on the road came down with asthma – an omen of what it will be like if I get to go there. Dr Aguilar was again brief and to the point: there's a job in the laboratory, but not unless all my papers are in order. Now that's what I'm caught up in. Señora de Holst has invited me to stay at her house; I'll probably go, but I haven't said anything definite yet. Tomorrow I'll stop living in poverty and work surrounded with blood. My aunt, Sara de la Serna, died of an embolism caused by an operation to remove a malignant tumour from her large intestine. I didn't love her, but her death has had an effect on me. She was a healthy, very active person who seemed as far as anyone could be from such a death. But it is a solution, since the disease would have left her in a state that would have been terrible for her.

A day completely lacking in movement. Haya de la Torre passed through Guatemala City. A letter arrived from Gualo in which he said that Big Rojo has been given a visa. Also a letter from Beatriz saying that another kilo of *mate* is on its way from Buenos Aires. Tomorrow I'll see the minister's secretary and find out what they have to say about the residence permit.

The days keep passing, but I no longer give a damn. Maybe one day I'll change my mind about the business with Helena Leiva, maybe not. But I know it will be settled somehow and I'm no longer racking my brains.

As for the jobs: nothing can be done about the residence permit until after Holy Week; the Health Minister said I should ask wherever I liked, and I know there is one at Livingston on the Atlantic coast. On Monday Helena will ask about that job for me. Hilda says she will ask about a job at the OAS. We'll see what comes of all this, but I don't have many illusions. My mind is made up, and one of these days I'll write to China and see what they have to say.

Nothing new under the sun.

On Sunday we went to the Children's City at San José Pinula. The name is a little pretentious, because there are only two little blocks housing forty kids, but it is still an interesting effort. The director is a lawyer, Orozco Posadas; he's half crazy, but what he has done is worthy of merit. The city is for reformatory children; they are given good food, good accommodation and school instruction, and are taught agricultural work and an occupation. The kids are delighted with it. As for my job prospects, the only new thing comes from Hilda's statistics professor, who works for the OAS, and from Núñez Aguilar who has promised to talk to the Minister for Foreign Affairs so that I get a residence permit.

The business with the professor is just words and nothing else. On returning from San Juan Sacatepéquez, we ran into a procession of hooded people with candles and scary faces carrying Christ on their backs. As we passed alongside, there was a moment when the men with spears gave us some ugly looks and I didn't like it at all.

We had to take a jeep to Guatemala City, which cost $5 for the eight of us. I spent the next day, today, writing, eating at de Holst's, playing canasta and looking through the gringo's books (all in English but very interesting). My progress in that language has not been enough for me to plunge into those hefty tomes, but I have a number of journals as well as Pavlov's physiology of the nervous system.

Several days have passed without anything to change this useless life. The gringo invited me to see a Russian film about Rimsky-Korsakov. Very fine music and thrilling singing by one of the women. But as always, the plot was slow and ponderous and the actors not very effective in their roles, except for the central character who was very natural.

My residence permit is still up in the air. Núñez Aguilar is moving and asking around, but I don't know if he'll be listened to – we shall see.

Núñez Aguilar is moving and asking around, but not too much. Nor am I doing a lot about it. Everything else is much the same, except that Hilda told me she is thinking of going to China, and added for one or two years. I advised her to think it over well. Of course she's in favour of leaving APRA. I'm still keeping to my eating rules. Mama writes that Sara left her 250,000 pesos in her will, which will certainly come in handy for her.

Days without any movement. I don't know what will happen; all that's certain is that I am alive and am not at all wasting the time. I received another kilo of *mate* from Buenos Aires. Of course it's different now that mother has "bread". I don't know how the residence business will work out – much the same, I suppose. Tomorrow I'll speak to Núñez Aguilar and see what has come of all this.

More days that aren't bringing anything new to Guatemala. With the residence permit, there are times when things get heavy and others when it seems I will get it. Morgan turned out to be useless. I went with the gringo to Chimaltenango on the Ministry of Education bus. A school was being given the name of Pedro Molina, Guatemala's great man. Don Adelberto said some fine words, but the guy who spoke from STEG did no more than repeat some commonplaces from the language of politicking.

My decision is made: unshakeable and heroic. If nothing has come of the residence permit within a fortnight, I'm going to bugger off from here. I'm thinking of making a game of it; I've already told the *pensión*, and I'll put everything in the right kind of safe place, in boxes that I'll ask Ernesto Weintaner for. Otherwise not much to report. We saw a performance of Sophocles's *Electra*, but it was very bad. A kilo of adrenalin that Alberto sent from Venezuela has arrived, as well as a letter asking me to go there – or rather, suggesting that I should go there. I don't feel like it much.

The remedies that Alberto sent from Venezuela are of sufficient quantity and quality, and that is enough by itself to raise my spirits. Meanwhile they have called me to the police – which is a step prior to residence. This comes after a siege at the ministry that was worse than Dien Bien Phu, whose fall strengthens my conviction that Asia will free itself from the colonialists.

My life is so exactly the same that it is hardly worth relating anything. On Monday I'm thinking of starting at Cardiolopina and la Halner, to have everything ready on Friday to leave here, which is paid up to Saturday. I don't think my affairs will be resolved before then, so I'll go to Quetzaltenango. I spend whatever time I can there and come back one day to speed things up, then go off again across country. We shall see (a formula I gave up some time ago).

The day is approaching when I'll take off somewhere. I've already burnt my bridges by announcing with a great fanfare that I'm leaving. If Lily's invitation is still on, I'll go to Quetzaltenango [. . .] if not, I'll head for the lake and try to go up some volcano. If none of that works out, I'll head for the Quiriguá area – if possible, with the gringo's camera. The residence business is at a standstill; I don't know when it will come through, nor do I care. Julia Mejías has given me a suitcase to fill with books and put into storage. I'll probably leave my clothes at the gringo's because Helena didn't say any more on the phone, so my luck has run out. News has come through which would suggest that the executive is going to issue new permits in a fortnight's time; it would be wonderful if it's true and they give me residence. I've heard from Buenos Aires that four kilos of *mate* are on their way to me by ship; they'll take a couple of months, but it doesn't matter, and they'll also send me *El Gráfico*. Nothing new in any other respect.

A lot of water has flowed under the bridge. I left the *pensión* on the appointed day, to the consternation of the whole family. The same day I went with Hilda to San Juan Sacatepéquez. [. . .] I slept all night there weathering the storms, with the rucksack in with me because I couldn't leave it out in the open. I had asthma on the way there, but was almost OK on the way back. Meanwhile the business pending at the Foreign Ministry was resolved, in the sense that I had to get out of the country. But Zochinson got me $20 and after a few days of sleeping in different places I headed for El Salvador.[40] At first I had problems at the border, but I found a way around them and in Santa Ana they gave me the right visa for six months in Guatemala. It looks as if this has solved some problems.

In El Salvador, I met a Mexican who was stranded at the border because of some trouble with his exit papers and had to return to San Salvador. We got quite friendly and he gave me his address in case I was ever in Mexico. I asked for a Honduran visa (which was supposed to come through Saturday evening), but I went to the port and stayed there Friday, Saturday and Sunday, so I don't know about the visa. In San Salvador I spoke to Hercilia's doctor friend, who did not recognize her as Señora Guevara and has just left with Hernández. Tomorrow, Monday, I'll go and see him for a while and

40 An undated letter (see p.56) explains to Ernesto's family the details of what happened. His father thinks it might be from April 1954.

51

then set off for Honduras or Guatemala, depending on whether they give me the visa or not. Life was very nice at the port, but I got sunburned and on the last day I could hardly bathe at all because it would have been criminal to go out in the sun.

I sent the diet packing and now the consequences can be seen. The route of my next journey will be decided tomorrow.

A day in San Salvador, a day not exactly of boredom but of disappointment, of anxiety posing as hunger, or maybe the other way round. There's no news from Honduras. I'm only going to wait until tomorrow, because my dollar reserves are used up. I met the Moreno couple, who were very nice and friendly, but they didn't invite me to eat. Tomorrow I'll give them a letter for Hercilia, as they are going to the United States next week. I spent the day reading an old history of El Salvador. I think I'll finish it tomorrow, and maybe then also go to the museum. I chucked the diet out of the window. We'll see what happens.

I delivered a letter for Hercilia to the Morenos and they invited me to eat with them. It wasn't a very big meal but enough to still my hunger. Then I took a minibus to Santa Ana, and from there to Chalchuapa and the ruins of Tazumal. But I found out that they were closed to the public, so I camped out in a strategic position beneath a lamp and started to read. After a while a lady caught on and offered me some hot water and a hammock to sleep in. As we spoke of Guatemala, I put my foot in it as usual and said there was more democracy there than in El Salvador, and it turned out that the master of the house was the town commandant.

The ruins of Tazumal are part of a huge complex stretching over several kilometres, though only the temples are still standing. There are traces of that mingling of Mayan civilization with the Tlascatelca conquerors which issued in the Mexican race. The main structure is a large quadrangular pyramid, which probably used to be crowned with a little pavilion. It is in the form of staircases made of stone and mud, which are covered with a

52

clayey mixture very similar to present-day cement. The whole thing does not have the solemnity of the Inca constructions. The only ornaments are two or three carvings, but the weather has completely worn them down so that they do not give us any clear idea of what the people were like who lived there.

The whole construction lay undiscovered for many years beneath a tree-covered mound of earth. In 1942 a North American archaeologist, Boxh, began the excavations, which have since continued with great success, despite meagre funding from the Salvadorean government. The building method appears to have been concentric, so that each new temple was larger and enclosed the one before it, lasting for an unknown period that may have been the 52 years of the Mayan century. There are 13 concentric layers, the last of which contains – in addition to the pyramid – a set of ball bearings and a semi-quadrangular setting. Beside the great pyramid, mainly Mayan in style, there is a much smaller one which has all the marks of being Mexican and which, despite its size, rose over the first. It too was probably crowned with a temple, although no traces remain of one. In the great pyramid, the final stages had no protection from the weather and suffered so badly that some have been almost completely lost. I left my address with the man in charge there and hitched a lift to San Salvador, as I had forgotten to pick up my exit permit there. Then I almost immediately got a minibus to Santa Techa, and from there hitched to Santa Ana just as night was falling. I slept at the highway exit close to the border.

I started walking early, but a jeep soon gave me a ride and then a car took me across the frontier and on to Progreso. From there I walked some 20 kilometres until a lorry picked me up and took me beyond Jalapa. It is a very beautiful region which rises gradually higher, filled with green pines and almost covered with low cloud. It had a special charm that I had not previously seen in Guatemala, although I don't rule out the possibility that it was because I hadn't been in that kind of situation before. I was already very tired when I began the descent on foot. My rucksack became leaden again and my briefcase made my fingers sore, so that as soon as night fell I staggered into the first house and asked them to put me up. There I pulled off the best deal of my whole trip when they swapped my good torch for one that was a load of rubbish – and I like a fool agreed to it.

I started sluggishly on my way, but my shoulders and feet slowed me right down. A lorry picked me up, but he charged me 40 cents to take me to Jalapa station, where I took the train to Progreso. A woman took pity on me there and gave me 25 cents. I set off on foot, but I had done no more than four kilometres when a jeep stopped and took me to El Ranchito, where the River Motagua is 100 metres wide and, owing to the altitude, quite torrential. I bathed in the river, washed my clothes and conditioned my feet with paper so that they would hold out a little longer. Then I walked another five kilometres or so until I reached a fairly deep river without a bridge. A lorry full of road workers picked me up and took me to Uzumatlán, where I slept the night. Here my stories were a bit on the tall side and I had to work hard to make the different versions fit together. The road to the Atlantic is quite far advanced, and all that is needed to make it passable are a few bridges – for at that time of the year the rivers are swollen and cannot always be forded.

I left early the next day and walked some 13 kilometres in the sun before flopping down and getting a lorry to take me to a station [. . .].[41] Then I caught a train to Quiriguá and went to see the ruins, which are about three kilometres from the station. The ruins are not important and consist of no more than a number of stelae and zoomorphic stones, with some polygonal stone shapes quite reminiscent of the lesser Inca ruins. In this type of construction, the Mayas did not come anywhere near the sophistication of the Incas, but a certain affinity between them is still discernible. Where you see a clear superiority over the Incas is in the size of the truly

41 Illegible in the original.

fascinating limestone figures, which are very reminiscent of the Hindu ruins in Asia. On one stele, in particular, a round-faced figure was wearing something like oriental trousers, and its knees were bent in a way that reminded me a lot of a Buddha. Another has the same facial features, ending in a triangular pear shape, rather like a beard of the Ho Chi Minh type. One of the zoomorphic stones has a whole number of sculptings or bas-reliefs which, according to the explanatory notice, are considered the highest point of indigenous American sculpture. Morley, however, has shown photographs of sculptures which seem to me superior. In any event, the landscape is deeply fascinating, with its silence, its large trees, and its grass that now grows on those esoteric stelae and the polished hieroglyphs you feel like touching. Were it not for the notices and the metal strip around each monument, you might think you had travelled on Brick Bradford's time machine. I slept on the station floor, protected from the mosquitoes by the bag that has come in very useful.

In the morning I presented myself to Dr Díaz. He is a reactionary Indian, but he treated me with the necessary courtesy and gave me something to eat at the hospital. A waiter, who was also the photographer for the whole area, accompanied me to the ruins and took six photos, charging me only for the film and giving me a few more pictures as a present. I was anyway very low on funds, although I still had enough to get back. Instead I decided to go straight to Puerto Barrios, but as the train was delayed by a fall of rocks I only arrived after 12.30 and slept in the station.

The next day, the tricky problem of finding work presented itself – but I found some on the Atlantic highway project. It involves working twelve hours at a stretch, from 6.00 in the evening to 6.00 in the morning, and it is quite a killer even for guys in better shape than I am. By 5.30 we were complete robots – or "ninepins", as they say here of drunks.

On the second day, the critical one, I worked much less heartily but still made it through to the end – which was a sign of what might follow.

But then one of the foremen offered to get me a railway pass; this is very good for them, because they pay for it only several days after the work is completed. The work is already lighter and, if it weren't for the mosquitoes (which are a real pain) and the lack of gloves (which turns your hands into sores), would be quite bearable. I spent the whole morning dozing in my "residence" by the sea, after a quick wash of my socks and shirts. I have become a real pig, full of dust and asphalt from the head down, but also contented. I have got the ticket. The old woman at whose place I had my meals told me to pay a dollar to her son in Guatemala. Anyway, I have proved to myself that I am capable of taking whatever comes – more, in fact, if it weren't for the asthma.

Now I am nicely settled on the train, feasting on a dollar that a semi-educated foreman gave me.

Letter to his mother

My dear mother,[42]

Don't think that my opening words are to keep Father happy; there really are signs that something is getting better and that my prospects are not so desperate at an economic level. I tell things tragically when that is the truth, and I assumed that Father considered me tough enough to endure whatever came my way, but if you prefer fairy tales I'll make up some very nice ones. In the days of silence my life has developed as follows. I went with a rucksack and a briefcase, half walking, half hitching, half (shame!) paying for shelter out of $10 that the government itself had given me. I reached El Salvador and the police confiscated some books I had brought from Guatemala, but I got through, obtained a visa (the right one this time) to enter Guatemala again, and went off to see the ruins left behind by some Mexicans, a branch of the Tlascaltecas,

42 This letter may date from the end of April 1954.

who once came south to conquer from their centre in Mexico and remained here until the arrival of the Spanish. The ruins are in no way comparable to the Mayan structures, still less the Incan. Then I spent a few days on the beach while awaiting a decision about the visa I had requested in order to visit some splendid ruins in Honduras. I slept in my bag on the seashore and no longer kept the strictest diet, but the healthiness of this life kept me in perfect shape – except for some blisters from the sun. I made friends with some guys who, as always in Central America, were travelling on alcohol, and, using the extrovertedness that comes with alcohol, I gave them a bit of my Guatemalan propaganda and recited some verses with a strong Colorado flavour. The upshot was that we all ended up in the police station, but they let us go after some advice from an important-looking officer to sing to the roses in the evening, and other jolly things like that. I preferred to vanish with a sonnet to thin air. The Hondurans refused me a visa just because I had residence in Guatemala, although I hardly need tell you of my good intention to see something of a strike that has broken out there and is supported by 25 per cent of the whole working population (a high figure anywhere, but especially in a country where there is no right to strike and only underground trade unions). The fruit company is in a fury, and of course Dulles and the CIA want to intervene in Guatemala because of its terrible crime in buying weapons from wherever it wishes (the United States has not sold it a single cartridge for some time now). [. . .]

Of course, I didn't consider the possibility of remaining there. I came back along half-abandoned roads with a big hole in my wallet, as a dollar isn't worth much more than a mango and you don't get anything great for 20. One day I walked nearly 50 kilometres (that would be lying but it was a lot), and after many days I came to the fruit company hospital where there are some small but beautiful ruins. Here I became completely convinced of what my American identity had refused to be convinced of: namely, that our forefathers were Asiatic (tell Father they will soon be demanding his paternal authority). Some bas-reliefs are the Buddha in person and – in all their characteristics – just like those of the old Hindu civilizations. It is a beautiful place, so beautiful that I committed the crime of Silvestre Bonard against my stomach and spent a dollar and a bit on some rolls of film and the hire of a camera. Then I begged some grub at the hospital, but I couldn't fill my bag with it more than half way up. I didn't have enough left to pay the train fare to Guatemala City, so I headed for Puerto Barrios and found some work there unloading barrels of tar at 2.63 for twelve hours' rock-hard labour, in a place where the mosquitoes swarm angrily in fabulous quantities. I ended up with my hands a mess and my back even worse, but nevertheless feeling quite happy. I worked from 6.00 in the evening till 6.00 in the morning and slept in an abandoned house on the seashore. Then I headed for Guatemala City and here I am with better prospects than before. [. .]

(my writing is not sloppy on purpose, but the result of four Cubans arguing next to me). [. . .]

The next will be calmer. I'll send you news if there is any. A hug for everyone.

Letter to his mother April 1954

Mother,

As you see, I didn't go to El Petén. The son of a bitch who was supposed to sign me up made me wait a month and then told me it wasn't on. [. . .]

I'd already presented him with a list of medicines, instruments and

"Che" (left) with Eduardo (Gualo) García, the Argentine law student with whom he travelled from Ecuador to Guatemala.

"Che" in Guatemala. Among the group are Ricardo Rojo, Luzmilla Oller, Eduardo (Gualo) García, Hilda Gadea and Oscar Valdovinos.

Mt Popocatepetl (5,340 m. high), the Aztec's "smoking mountain",
is a volcano. It last erupted in 1920.

"Che" (right), with a group of friends, during one of his attempts
to climb Mt Popocatepetl.

The ascent of Mt Popocatepetl.

The cathedral at Campeche, Mexico, seen from the market place.

"Che", photographed in Campeche.

The Observatory at Chichén-Itzá.

The temple of Indovino at Uxmal, photographed recently by
"Che"'s son, Ernesto Guevara March.

Two photographs of "Che" taken during his time in Mexico.

"Che" (centre) with Reinaldo Benítez Nápoles, Alberto Bayo and Universo Sánchez at the Miguel E. Schulz 136 prison.

"Che" (foreground) in the Miguel E. Schulz 136 prison with a group of people who would later take part in the "Granma" expedition, leading to the overthrow of the Cuban dictator, Fulgencio Batista, and the emergence of Fidel Castro as the leader of the Cuban people.

"Che" (centre) with two unidentified acquaintances.

the rest, and had become strong on diagnosis of the main tropical diseases in the area. Of course this will be useful to me anyway, especially as I now have a chance of working for the fruit company in a banana-growing area.

What I don't want to miss is a visit to the ruins of El Petén. There is a wonderful city there, Tical, and a much less important one, Piedras Negras, where the art of the Mayas nevertheless reached an extraordinary level. The museum here has a lintel which, though completely broken, is a genuine work of art in world terms.

My old Peruvian friends lacked a feeling for the tropics, so they weren't able to do anything similar; besides they didn't have the easy-to-work limestone that you find in these parts. I am more and more happy to have left. My medical culture is not increasing greatly, and I am absorbing other knowledge that interests me much more. [. . .]

I would like to pay them a visit, but I have no idea when or how. To speak of plans in my situation would be to tell of a hastily assembled dream. Anyway if I get the job at the fruit company, and only then, I intend to concentrate on settling the debts I have here and the ones I left there, to buy myself the camera, to visit El Petén, and to take myself off north in Olympic style – that is, north to Mexico.

I'm glad you have such a high opinion of me. Anyway it would be very difficult for anthropology to be my sole occupation in my mature years. It seems to me rather paradoxical that the lodestar of my life could be the study of what is now dead beyond recall. I am sure of two things. First, if I reach the genuinely creative period of life around the age of 35, my exclusive occupation, or anyway my main one, will be nuclear physics, genetics or another area that combines some of the most interesting parts of subjects with which I am familiar. Second, the American continent will be the theatre of my adventures much more than I would previously have thought;

I really think I have grown to understand it and I feel American as distinct from any other people on earth. Naturally I shall visit the rest of the world. [. . .]

There's little I can say of my daily life that would interest you. In the morning I go to the health department and work a few hours at the laboratory; in the afternoon I go and study at a library or museum; in the evening I read medicine or something else, write a letter finally, and attend to domestic tasks. I drink *mate* when there is any, and I engage in endless discussions with the comrade Hilda Gadea, an *aprista*[43] whom I try to persuade in my gentle way to leave that dump of a party. She has a heart of platinum, at least. Her help is felt in everything to do with my daily life (beginning with the *pensión*).

Days have passed in which things have and have not happened. I have a firm promise of a job as assistant to a medical practitioner. I returned my dollar. I again visited Obdulio Barthe, the Paraguayan, who told me off for the way I was behaving and admitted that he thought I was an agent from the Argentine embassy. In fact I learnt that this, or something like it, is a widespread suspicion. But the Honduran leader Ventura Ramos doesn't think so. As the row with Mrs Horst is still continuing, I smuggle myself in once a day and sleep in the room of Ñico the Cuban, who kills himself laughing all day without doing anything much. Ñico leaves on Monday, so then I'll move to the room of a Guatemalan friend called Coca. A Cuban who sings tangos sleeps in the same room as Ñico; he invited me to hike south with him down to Venezuela, and I'd go if it weren't for the job they've promised me. They say they'll give me the residence permit and Zochinson has moved to become head of immigration. [. . .]

Once more the days pass without anything new. I am at the *pensión*

43 That is: a member of APRA.

sharing with the Cuban songbird, now that Ñico has left for Mexico. I go one day after another about the job, but there's nothing. Now they've told me to leave it for this week, and I don't really know what to do. I don't know whether the comrades are still set on my not getting something or not. Not much news comes from Buenos Aires. Helena is leaving for an unknown destination and I've stopped looking, but she will take me to the house of an aunt who'll give me lunch. She'll also speak to the minister over the phone. I have a good old attack of asthma, brought on by what I've been eating the last few days. I hope it will pass if I go on a strict diet for three days.

Letter to his mother 10 May 1954

Mother,

[. . .]

I think of the future with pleasant feelings; my residence permit is going ahead, if slowly, as is the way in these parts. I reckon that in a month from now I'll be able to go to the cinema without being trailed by some good-natured fellow. I have been promised something that I think I've already told Father about, and I've also mentioned my plans to him rather perfunctorily. I've decided to leave this *pensión* on the 15th and sleep in the open air in a bag I've inherited from a compatriot who was passing through. Like that I'll be able to see all the places I want, except for El Petén because the rainy season makes it impossible to go there. I'll be able to go up a volcano, as I've wanted for a long time to see the tonsils of Mother Earth (what a nice image). This is the land of the volcanoes, and there are some to suit everyone's taste. My own tastes are simple – neither too high nor too active. I could become very rich in Guatemala, but by the low method of ratifying my title, opening a clinic and specializing in allergies (it's full of tell-tale colleagues here). To do that would be the most horrible betrayal of the two I's struggling inside me: the socialist and the traveller. [. . .]

Warm and moist hugs because here it is raining all day (as long as the *mate* lasts – very romantic).

The latest events belong to history – a quality which I think is appearing for the first time in my notes. A few days ago, some aircraft from Honduras crossed the border with Guatemala and flew over the city in broad daylight, machine-gunning people and military objectives. I enlisted in the health brigades to help on the medical side and in the youth brigades that patrol the streets by night. The course of events was as follows. After the aircraft had passed, troops under the command of Colonel Castillo Armas, a Guatemalan émigré in Honduras, crossed the frontier at several points and advanced on the town of Chiquimula. The Guatemalan government, which had already protested to Honduras, let them enter without offering any resistance and presented its case to the United Nations.

Colombia and Brazil, two docile Yankee instruments, put forward a plan to pass the matter to the OAS. The USSR rejected this and was in favour of ordering a ceasefire. The invaders failed in their attempt to use aircraft gunfire to get the masses to rise up, but they did capture the town of Bananera and cut the railway to Puerto Barrios. The aim of the mercenaries was clear enough: to take Puerto Barrios and bring in all kinds of weapons and further mercenary troops. This became apparent when the schooner *Siesta de Trujillo* was captured trying to unload weapons at that port. The final offensive collapsed, but in the midland towns the attackers committed acts of real barbarism, murdering members of SETUFCO[44] at the cemetery by throwing a hand grenade at their chest.

The invaders thought that if they just gave a shout, the whole people would come out and follow them – and for this purpose they parachuted in weapons. But in fact the people immediately rallied under the command of Arbenz. The invading troops were checked and defeated on all fronts and

44 The United Fruit Company Workers Union.

driven back past Chiquimula, near the Honduran frontier. Pirate aircraft flying from bases in Honduras and Nicaragua continued to machine-gun the fronts and towns. Chiquimula was heavily bombed, and several people were wounded and a little girl of three killed as a result of the bombing of Guatemala City.

My life has been like this: first I reported to the youth brigades of the Alliance, where I spent several days at a central assembly point until the Health Ministry sent me to be billeted at the Maestro Health Centre. I volunteered for the front, but they didn't pay me a blind bit of notice.

Letter to his mother 20 June 1954

Dear Mother,

This letter will reach you a little after your birthday, which you will perhaps spend a little uneasily on my account. Let me tell you that although there is nothing to fear at the moment, the same cannot be said of the future – although personally I have the sense of being inviolable (inviolable is not the right word but perhaps my subconscious played a trick on me). The situation may be summarized as follows.

Five or six days ago the first pirate aircraft from Honduras flew over Guatemala, without doing anything. On the next and the following days they bombed a number of military installations in Guatemala, and two days ago a warplane machine-gunned the lower parts of the city and killed a girl of two. The incident served to unite all Guatemalans behind their government and all those who, like myself, came here attracted by the country. At the same time, mercenary troops led by an ex-colonel who was dismissed from the army some time ago for treason left Tegucigalpa, the capital of Honduras, and crossed the frontier quite deeply into Guatemala. The government, acting with great caution so that the United States could not declare

Guatemala the aggressor, limited itself to protesting to Tegucigalpa and sending all the information to the Security Council of the United Nations; it allowed the attacking forces to advance sufficiently so that there would not be any so-called border incidents. Colonel Arbenz has got guts, there's no doubt about that, and is prepared to die at his post if necessary. His latest speech did no more than reaffirm this fact, which we all knew already, and spread calm in the country. The danger does not come from the small number of troops that have entered the country so far, nor from the warplanes that have bombed civilian homes and machine-gunned a number of people; the danger lies in how the gringos (in this case the Yankees) are manipulating their stooges at the United Nations, since even a vague declaration would be of great help to the attackers. The Yankees have finally dropped the good-guy mask that Roosevelt gave them and are now committing outrages in these parts. If things reach the point where it is necessary to fight planes and modern troops sent by the fruit company or the USA, then that is what will be done. The people's spirits are very high, and the shameless attacks, together with the lies in the international press, have united behind the government all those who used to be politically indifferent. There is a real climate of struggle. I myself have been assigned to emergency medical service and have also enrolled in the youth brigades to receive military instruction for any eventuality. I don't think the big explosion will come, but we shall see after the meeting of the Security Council, which is scheduled, I think, for tomorrow. Anyway, by the time this letter arrives, you will know what is to be expected.

For the rest, there's not much news. As the Argentine embassy has not been functioning these days, I haven't had any news since a letter from Beatriz and another from you last week.

I have been told they are on the point of giving me the job at the Health Department, but the offices have been busy with all the commotion and it seemed a little unwise to go bothering them about my little job when they are involved with much more important things.

Well, Mother, I hope you had the happiest birthday possible after this troubled year. I'll send news as soon as I can. Chau,

The minister came here today, Saturday, 26 June, while I was away seeing Hilda; she gave me a lot of stick because I was thinking of asking him to send me to the front. [. . .]

A terrible cold shower has fallen on all those who admire Guatemala. On the night of Sunday, 27 June, President Arbenz unexpectedly announced that he was resigning. He publicly denounced the fruit company and the United States as being directly behind all the bombing and strafing of the civilian population.

An English merchant ship has been bombed and sunk in the port of San José, and the bombing continues. At this moment Arbenz has announced his decision to place the command in the hands of Colonel Carlos Enrique Díaz. He said that he was motivated by his desire to save the October revolution and to stop the North Americans from coming to this land as masters. Colonel Díaz said nothing in his speech. The PDR and PRG both expressed their agreement and called on their members to cooperate with the new government. The other two parties, the PRN and PGT,[45] said nothing. I went to sleep with a feeling of frustration about what has happened. I had again spoken to the Health Ministry and asked to be sent to the front. Now I don't know what to do. We'll see what today brings.

Two days thick with political events, although they did not mean much for me personally. The events: Arbenz resigned under pressure from a North American military mission that was threatening massive bombing and a declaration of war by Honduras and Nicaragua provoking United

45 PGT: the Guatemalan Labour Party.

States intervention. But Arbenz may not have foreseen what happened next. On the first day Colonels Sánchez and Fejo Monzón (a well-known anti-Communist) joined forces with Díaz, and their first decree made the PGT illegal. The persecution began at once and the embassies filled up with people seeking asylum. But worse came early the next day, when Díaz and Sánchez resigned, leaving Monzón as head of government with two lieutenant-colonels under him. They completely caved in to Castillo Armas (or so it is said), and martial law provisions were decreed for anyone found carrying prohibited-calibre weapons. My own situation is roughly that I will be expelled from the small hospital where I am now, probably tomorrow following my reclassification as a *"chebol"*.[46] Repression is coming. Ventural and Amador are seeking asylum, H. is keeping at home, Hilda has changed her address, Núñez is at home. The top people in the Guatemalan party are seeking asylum. It is said that Castillo will enter the city tomorrow; I have received a nice letter that I'll keep here for my grandchildren.

Several days have passed in which things did not happen at the feverish pace of the previous days. Castillo Armas won a complete victory. The junta is made up of Fejo Monzón as president plus Castillo Armas, Cruz, Dubois and Colonel Mendoza. Within a fortnight there will be an election within the junta to decide who is boss; Castillo Armas, of course. There is no Congress and no Constitution. They have shot the judge of Salamá, Ramiro Reyes Flores, after he killed a guard who was trying to trick him. Edelberto Torres has been arrested and charged with being a Communist; who knows what will be the poor old man's fate. Today, 3 July, the "liberator" Castillo Armas entered the city to great acclamation. I am living in the house of two Salvadorean women who have sought asylum abroad – one in Chile, the other in Brazil – together with an old woman who is always going on about her husband's misdeeds and other such interesting matters. They have sent me packing from the hospital and I've settled in here . . .

46 A reversal of *bolche,* or "bolshy".

Letter to his mother 4 July 1954

Mother,

It has all been like a beautiful dream from which you are in no hurry to awake. Reality is knocking on many doors, and the volleys rewarding the most fervent support for the old regime are beginning to be heard. Treason continues to be the birthright of the army, and once more the aphorism is confirmed that sees the liquidation of the army as the true principle of democracy (if the aphorism does not exist, *I* believe it). [. . .]

The harsh truth is that Arbenz did not know how to rise to the occasion. This is how it all happened.

After the aggression began from Honduras, without anything like a declaration of war (indeed, with protests about alleged border violations), the planes came to bomb the city. We were completely defenceless, since there were no planes, no anti-aircraft guns and no shelters. Some people were killed – not many. But panic gripped the people, especially "the brave and loyal army of Guatemala". A North American military mission met the president and threatened him with real bombing that would reduce Guatemala City to ruins, and with a declaration of war by Nicaragua and Honduras that the United States would join under its mutual-aid pacts with those countries. The military got the wind up and issued an ultimatum to Arbenz.

Arbenz did not think to himself that the city was full of reactionaries, and that the destroyed homes would belong to them rather than to the mass of the population, who own nothing and were defending the government. And although Korea and Indochina are there as examples, he did not think to himself that a people in arms is an invincible power. He could have given arms to the people but he did not want to – and now we see the result.

I already had my little job but I lost it at once, so now I am as I was at the beginning, though without debts because I decided to cancel them for reasons of *force majeure*. I live comfortably thanks to the kindness of a good friend, and I do not want for anything. I don't know anything about my future, except that I'll probably go to Mexico. A little shamefully, I have to tell you that I have thoroughly enjoyed myself during these days. That magical sense of invulnerability about which I told you in another letter made me lick my chops when I saw people run madly as soon as the planes appeared or, at night, when the blacked-out city was filled with gunfire. Let me say in passing that the light bombers have an imposing quality. I watched one make for a target quite close by: you could see the machine growing larger every moment as little tongues of fire intermittently issued from its wings; and you could hear the sounds of its shrapnel and the firing of its light machine-guns. For a moment it hung horizontally in the air before zooming down and making the earth shake from the impact of its bomb load. Now all this has passed, and all you hear are the rockets of the reactionaries who have emerged ant-like from the ground to celebrate victory and are looking for Communists to string up (which is what they call anyone from the previous government). The embassies are filled to the brim, and ours and the Mexican one are the worst. A lot of sport is made with all this, but it is pretty clear that the few fat cats can be easily tricked.

If you want to have some idea of where this government is heading, let me mention a couple of points. One of the first villages that fell belonged to the fruit company, whose workers were on strike at the time. The invaders immediately declared the strike at an end, took the leaders to the cemetery, and killed them by throwing hand grenades at their chest. One night a flare shone out from the cathedral into the darkened city just as a plane was flying overhead.

The first act of thanksgiving was given by the bishop; the second by Foster Dulles, who is the fruit company's lawyer. Today, 4 July, there is a solemn mass with all the paraphernalia, and every paper is congratulating the United States government in outlandish terms on the occasion of its national day.

Mother, I'll have to see how I am going to send you these letters. If I put them in the mail they'll ruin my nerves (the president said – up to you whether you believe it – that this was a country with strong nerves). A big hug to you all.

The business with the asylum-seekers remains the same as before. The novelty has worn off and everything is calm. Helena left today by plane. The German has a worse and worse look in his eyes when he sees me. I'll visit him only once to pick up some things and the books I left there.

Some quite serious things have been happening, though not in the political order, where the only change is that illiterates have been denied the right to vote. In a country where 65 per cent of the adult population is illiterate, this means reducing the number of those who vote to 35 per cent. Of those 35, perhaps 15 are in favour of the regime – and so the level of fraud does not have to be very high for the likely "people's candidate", Carlos Castillo Armas, to be elected. The serious thing is that I have been told to leave the house where I have been living, since Yolanda, the other sister of the women in exile, is here and is planning to move home to San Salvador. I'll see if I can go to the house of Helena's aunt.

Here I am settled in the new house. I have been going as always to Argentine embassy, but today it was closed down. Still, I was able to enter in the evening because today was 9 July.[47] There is a new ambassador, Torres Gispena, a stocky little pedant from Córdoba. I ate a number of little things but not a lot of each. The things I have to put up with! I met some

47 Argentina's national day.

interesting people at the embassy: one of them, Aguilez, has written a book on Land Reform; another, Dr Díaz, is a Salvadorean paediatrician and a friend of Romero from Costa Rica.

The asthma is screwing me up because of what I ate at the embassy. Otherwise nothing much has changed. I got a letter and a photo from my mother, and a letter from Celia and Tita Infante.

El Cheché[48] must have been given asylum just now, because we had agreed that he would present himself at the embassy at 6.30. My plans are very uncertain, but I'll most likely go to Mexico – although I am also weighing the possibility of chancing my luck in Belize.

Belize is a long way from here. But whether it's near or far, I'm at one of those moments – I don't know why – when a bit of lateral pressure can send me off in a completely different direction. If everything works out OK, I'll soon be safe and sound in the embassy, because I have already asked for and been granted asylum. On one of the many days I went there, when I had just finished the article and was thinking of going to Hilda's, I came across a girl (the landlady's daughter at the *pensión* where Hilda was staying) who told me that liberation-army soldiers had come and taken away the landlady and Hilda. They soon released the landlady, but Hilda is still being detained. I was at a loss for a few days, but in the end I took refuge and here I am enjoying fresh food in the company of a motley group of people including, most notably, El Cheché.

Several days of asylum have passed. It would appear that Hilda has been released, as the paper reported that she had gone on hunger strike and the minister had promised to release her two days ago. The asylum can't be described as boring but it is sterile; the numbers of people here mean that you can't spend your time doing what you want. My asthma is bad and I feel like getting the hell out of here, but they're giving me problems with the visa for Mexico. Hilda doesn't come here. I don't know if this is because

48 José Manuel Vega Suárez, a Cuban exile living in Guatemala.

she doesn't know where I am but is able to visit me, or because she is not able to visit me. If there is no great danger, I'll leave here and toddle off to Lake Atitlán. Nothing has been happening politically, except that Decree No. 900 on the Land Reform has been declared unconstitutional.

Several more days have passed in rather sterile surroundings. All those who have taken refuge here are quite good people; the most interesting is Pellecer. I already have my special (or more or less special) food, and I sunbathe every morning, so I am in no hurry to leave. I don't know anything at all about Hilda. I sent her a message but got nothing back in reply; I don't know if it reached her. The political situation hasn't changed, except that there is more in the way of persecution. I had a discussion with Pellecer on Arbenz's decision to give up the presidency. I don't think that he himself has a very clear idea of whether the situation has turned out in the best possible way. I don't think so.

Several more days of confinement, marked by a deep sense of boredom, regular attacks of asthma, two broken sprays and a search for the ones that were in Helena's house, the surprising discovery that she has arrived in Guatemala. Life is monotonous and undisciplined, with pointless discussions and every possible form of time-wasting.

The main event was the sound of continuous gunfire from dawn on Monday. It was hard to imagine what was happening, but the rumours that gradually began to circulate made it possible to build up a picture of reality: a parade of regular soldiers and liberation-army troops yesterday had the effect of humiliating the regular army; then some members of the liberation army denigrated some army cadets, and that was enough to trigger an explosion. At first it was only the cadets against the liberation army, but as the day wore on the whole army swung over to the cadets, though not as energetically as it might. The upshot was that the cadets made the liberation army surrender and march through the city with their hands in the air. At that point the army was in complete control and there was some attempt at a coup d'état, but as always the soldiers lacked resolve. The next day, Castillo Armas gave an incoherent speech drooling stupidities, and the people jeered at the name of Monzón, but by the time he appeared the air base had swung round again and he was in control of the situation. He took some soldiers prisoner, and again a vociferous anti-Communism was unleashed with the support of the reactionaries. One has the impression that Castillo Armas's success in maintaining himself is due to Yankee support and to the instability and indecision of people in the army. Nothing new has been heard about any safe-conducts; my name is not on the list of those given asylum.

Several more days of my featureless stay at the embassy have passed. The Castillo Armas government has been completely consolidated. They took a number of soldiers prisoner, and that was the end of it. The shared sleeping with various people in the chancellery means that I have made a superficial analysis of each one of them. I shall begin with Carlos Manuel Pellecer. From what I have been able to gather, he was a student at the Polytechnic in the Ubico period and was tried and expelled. He went to Mexico, then showed up as an attaché at Guatemalan embassies in Britain and Europe – by which time he was a Communist. Here in Guatemala he was a deputy and a peasant leader at the time of Arbenz's fall. He is an intelligent and seemingly brave man. He has great influence over all the comrades who have taken refuge here, and I am not sure whether it is due to his personality or to the fact that he was a top Party leader. He always stands straight, with his feet together, as if at attention. He wrote a book of verse in years gone by – a common malady in this part of the world. His Marxist education is not as solid as that of other figures I have known, and he conceals it beneath a certain petulance. The impression he gives me is of a sincere but excitable individual, one of those ambitious people who, as the result of a blunder, can find himself in the position of violently abjuring his faith, but who, at a certain moment, is capable of making the most exalted sacrifices.

In other conversations, he made me aware that he is completely on top of the agrarian question.

Another day in the series, with a report that 120 certificates are shining in the distance, due to be issued later this week. That doesn't affect me, but I am eagerly awaiting Hilda's arrival, having sent for her so that I can see what is happening outside. Today's analysis is of Mario de Armas. He is a Cuban, a member of the orthodox party founded by Chibás, and not an anti-Communist. A simple guy, he was a railwayman in Cuba and took part in the abortive assault on the Moncada Barracks. He took refuge in the Guatemalan Embassy and then came here. Without political training of any kind, he is your average happy-go-lucky Cuban. But he is a good comrade and you can tell he is honest.

Yesterday it was announced that safe-conducts will be given to foreigners, so a real riot has been taking shape. A chess competition has begun in which I won the first two games, one against one of the best four players (myself included). An average player beat the one I was most afraid of, so that leaves two of us quite well placed.

Today it's José Manuel Vega Suárez, alias Cheché: a Cuban, as rough as an old shell-case, who lies like they do in Andalusia. I don't know anything for sure about his life in Cuba, but there are signs that he played the "funny guy" and that Batista's police gave him a real beating and threw him on a railway line. He was anti-Communist. Here he keeps us amused with his unspiteful exaggerations. He's like a big child, selfish and bad-mannered, who thinks that everyone should submit to his whims. He eats like a *biguá*.[49]

The issuing of safe-conducts has been announced: it will include the two Cubans and the Nicaraguan engineer Santos Benatares, an expert on the United States who was, I know, part of the Nicaraguan leadership in exile. Another Nicaraguan, Fernando Lafuente, said on being arrested that a Nicaraguan engineer could give a reference on his behalf; they asked him if

49 A water bird found in the River Plate area.

he was an expert on the United States, he said yes, and without further ado was thrown into jail. He was released at the time of Arbenz's fall, but he now had the reputation (rather hastily assigned, in my view) of being a spy. He has proven to be an intelligent person, to some extent a Marxist, perfectly at home with the panorama of world events. He is a sceptic, not a fighter. His attitude keeps wavering, and I don't think it's because of too much analysis. He's a good comrade, meticulous like a good engineer, but a little dull because his mania for analysis carries him to extremes even in matters of little account. His analysis of surplus value was interesting; I must consider the point more closely.

Everything is devilishly complicated. I don't know how the hell I'm going to get out of here, but I'll manage it somehow. I got a letter from Hilda in which she said that Helenita Leiva is under arrest. In a way I'm glad to hear this, because it means there won't be suspicions about her (the Communists thought she was suspicious). Meanwhile the safe-conducts have been arriving. Roberto Castañeda is a Guatemalan photographer, though hardly brilliant at his occupation, as well as being a ballet dancer. He strikes me as a person with an artistic temperament, clear-sighted intelligence, and a desire to be perfect in everything he does. He has travelled behind the Iron Curtain and is a sincere admirer of everything there, although he hasn't joined the Party. He lacks knowledge of Marxist theory and perhaps would not be a good militant because of those, let's say, bourgeois defects. But it's certain that he would be in there when the time came for action. He seems a wonderful personality in his relationships, and he has virtually none of the effeminate characteristics of a ballet dancer.

Another day added to the collection, without any greater victories over my reputation for idling. Florencio Méndez: member of the PGT. He was in Chiquimula with the government troops when the town fell through the treachery of its defenders – or rather, through the treachery of those commanding the defence. He is a simple guy, with no great culture or intelligence. His Marxist culture is nil and he behaves like a simple machine obeying slogans. He is a happy-go-lucky sort who probably has a congenital defect, since here in our refuge he has a brother on the borderline of oligophrenia. Obviously brave and loyal, he could – in his carefree, robot-like efficiency – reach the heights of sacrifice for an ideal.

Another two days without anything much to add to the general points made before. Luis Arturo Pineda: a 21-year-old Guatemalan, member of the PGT. He's a serious kid, proud of his effectiveness as a militant and firmly convinced of the Party's infallibility. His greatest ambition would be to become Party secretary in Guatemala, or perhaps the whole of Latin America, and to shake hands with Malenkov. From his position of militant orthodoxy, he looks out with contempt at everything that is not subject to Party discipline. He thinks he is very intelligent but in fact he isn't – though he is far from stupid either. His commitment makes him prepared for any kind of sacrifice for the Party.

Two more days have passed in which the only distraction has been to wait for Hilda to arrive. She came to the door twice, but was not able to get in. I'm not very well because of my asthma, so I'll take a purge and then fast tomorrow. Felicito Alegría: he's a quiet, humble guy, so withdrawn that I cannot judge his degree of intelligence. He gives the impression of being a shock element, with high fighting capacities and great solidity. Marco Tulio de la Roca: a 20-year-old Guatemalan; he apparently writes poetry, but has not shown any sign of it here. He's serious and also quiet, but he has a rather sad smile expressing a fatalistic and thinking brain. I don't think he is politically active as a militant.

Hercilia has written from New York in answer to a letter of mine; she tells me about the business with María Luisa, which seems to be serious. Today's portrait is of Gillete, quite a daring kid, I think. He's somewhere around 18 to 20, apparently without any great intellectual qualities. Good and simple. His characteristic is to write reams of verse, whose content I do not know but I imagine to be bad. He comes out with some fairly clever remarks, such as "this dying every day is quite a common sight" – which he uses to criticize another young poet in our refuge. I haven't talked with him enough to form a clear view about how much he knows or about his poetic talents.

Another day wasted. Marco Antonio Sandoval: an 18-year-old Guatemalan student and poet. As a poet, he is plagued by Neruda-esque features and meditations on death, but he occasionally comes up with a fine image. His character is full of romantic imagery, and he has developed into an energetic admirer of himself. He speaks with remarkable seriousness about everything concerning himself and speaks with great assurance about certain things. He has a caustic character, but lacks the nerve for sustained repartee. He has no political formation and takes everything as a political experience.

No news in two new days. I had a go at cooking, and although I managed it my muscles were tired by the end – which shows my lack of physical fitness. Núñez Aguilar leaves today for Argentina; I gave him my father's address, maybe he'll speak to him. Valdez – I don't remember his first name – is another of the young poets in the group. I've only read one of his compositions; it's in free verse and has a marked social-struggle content, but without the spark that distinguishes a real poet. He is 18 years old, with a roguish, ill-bred character typical of his age, despite the germs of something more serious. He is an open and forthright character, without great political ambitions but capable of acquiring them in time.

Another day wasted without anything new. Marco Antonio Derdon, alias Terremoto: a kid with few intellectual gifts and a physique indicating a degree of hypophyseal or hypogenital infantilism, as confirmed by the fact that, while we were in the refuge, one of his testicles moved up at the same time that he suffered an indirect inguinal hernia. He has no other appeal than his pathological constitution, for it is impossible to speak of any political formation in his case.

Another day of absolute nullity. One international event disturbing the monotony of the days has been the suicide of President Vargas. It has left me feeling a little disconcerted, because I don't know what path the vice-president, or those behind him, will impress upon Brazil. In any event, I suspect that tumultuous days lie ahead for the Brazilian people. Locally, a refugee has escaped by jumping over the wire on the wall. Hugo "Old Woman" Blanco, a young poet. A bad poet. I don't even think he is intelligent. Helpfulness seems to be the feature that marks him all over. The smile of a good little boy is always there accompanying the poet.

Yet another without anything new. Alfonso Riva Arroyo: leader of the healthworkers' union and an interesting person because of his intellectual scruples. He has a certain Marxist way of looking at things and is in open conflict with the Communists. He also has insomnia, which I imagine to be psychological in origin. He is a carpenter – a good one, he says. I gave him a letter for my father. This completes my account of people in the main hall of the chancellery.

Two or three days in which a lot of time has passed and one important general measure has been introduced. Perón has agreed that families can be taken as well. This changes the horizon for many of the refugees: one man, for example, decided to give himself up to the police because he didn't want to be separated from his family, and after telling people the day before did actually leave and give himself up, but the police wanted to play games and refused either to take him away or to let him go, so that he spent a good few hours outside with the wife and children who had come to say goodbye to him. In the end the minister got tired of it all and let him go inside to sleep; then at 2.00 in the morning the news came that he would be allowed to leave with his whole family. The next night, something less spectacular but no less important occurred. Victor Manuel Gutiérrez entered by one of the garden walls and was given asylum, but at 2.00 the main wing was reinforced so that no-one else could enter. Raúl Salazar: a typographer aged about 30, simple way of thinking, perhaps subnormal, who devotes himself to his work and nothing else, but was all the same of some importance in the PGT. He was on the People's Court and a union leader – a docile one, I should imagine.

Some jolly things have happened in the last two days. Gutiérrez's arrival caused great alarm in the embassy, where an imprudent phrase was used by one of the Pinedas about Perón's demagogy in giving asylum to the exiles' families as a pretext to shit all over the Communists – and on Pellecer when he tried to explain things. Afterwards, they confined thirteen of us to the garage and forbade us to speak with the rest, while at the same time they isolated Pellecer and Gutiérrez in a room by themselves. As if in answer to this, the two younger Pinedas escaped the same night.

It was very funny to see the face with which Banabés, protected by the fury of officialdom, expressed his own fury as well. I'll continue with that group at the same time as the thirteen. Now there are Lencho Méndez, Luis Arturo Pineda, Roberto Castañeda, Cheché Vega and myself, leaving eight. Humberto Pineda, elder brother of the other one, has a similar psychological make-up, but the elder seems better and generally well disposed, though just as restless as his brother. They've certainly got their heads screwed on. José Antonio Ochoa – a typographer, a union leader with a consistent line, though not a member of any party – belongs to the group of thirteen. His character is gentle, with the same consistency as his plumpish body, but he has a clear mind and is most consistent in his political line. He is a cheerful character, expressive and playful, a little childlike and sometimes inclined to be a little sad. He would not be capable of any heroic action, but he is incapable of treachery.

As if in response to what I was saying, Ochoa has managed to get transferred to the other side and is now calm and contented there. Now ten are left in the lock-up.

Ricardo Ramírez is perhaps one of the most capable leaders of the youth movement. Obviously the Party has replaced the home he does not seem to have had in his youth – or rather, in his childhood, as he is only 23 now. He is going to Buenos Aires, where of course his experience in the Party will come in handy. His general culture is high and his way of tackling problems much less dogmatic than that of other comrades. Of those from the chancellery, the one missing from the picture I have been describing is Arana, an old typographer aged about 50, weak and lacking ideological foundations but loyal to the Party. A man of average intelligence, he is sufficiently capable to realize that the only ideal road for the working class is Communism.

Several days have passed without anything new, except that Cheché caused a row with a little whore of a maid and they have shut us up more firmly still. Another of "the thirteen": Faustino Fermán Tino, a shoemaker. A simple way of thinking but as loyal and sincere as anyone could be; a cheerful and even-keeled character; technically very gifted as a shoemaker; those are his main features. Tomás Yancos, one of the old comrades from the chancellery, is an enigmatic personality. Like Rivas Arroyo, who later turned out a traitor, he seems to have been one of those who had "some differences" with the Party, though they were compatible with the general line. This is wrong, and Yancos turned out to be a son of a bitch. He has a strange character, with a brusqueness that puts people off, but he often seems to be in jest. His character is generally unpleasant.

Several days have passed, and things of greater or lesser importance have occurred which I have already forgotten. One that stands out, however, is the flight of Lencho Méndez and Roberto Murailles. Roberto seemed to be a pretty wild fellow, completely impulsive and without any intellectual foundation. One can be certain of his loyalty but not, I think, of anything else.

The next day, 118 refugees left in the five aeroplanes that came to take them. Among them were Carlos Manuel Pellecer and Victor Manuel Gutiérrez. The embassy has remained empty; only I am left of the group of thirteen from the kennels.

I spoke to Sánchez Toranzo and will be getting out today. Varisco, a friend of Gualo García's, came on the plane and brought me from home $150, two suits, four kilos of *mate* and a whole load of useless things.

Of those left from the thirteen, I have not yet analysed "Figaro" Vázquez, the hairdresser, a man without much of an intellectual foundation but with great pretensions. He doesn't seem a bad type, but he operates through repeated impulses not with revolutionary continuity; he is very ostentatious in everything he does and also quite stormy. It was he who sowed a note of discord in the friendly atmosphere of the thirteen.

Humberto Pineda was recognized by us and the embassy as the leader of the whole group. He is a man who has given up his violent impulses (like those of his sons) for a calmer and more reasonable attitude. His intellectual capacities are not too great, nor his intellectual formation, but he is able to rise to what is expected of him; he is a good militant. Eduardo Contreras is a teacher, small in size and quite young in age, a very fine person, cheerful and playful, with something of a theoretical foundation and a very good practical basis. Brave and loyal. Sometimes he seems a little pedantic, but it is a harmless and not unpleasant kind of pedantry.

I walked free without any problem and immediately paid my first visit – and a really passionate one it was. I went to sleep at old Mrs Leiva's and visited F.U., who didn't send me the article, so there is nothing concrete against me. Today I'll see about getting my passport, and if there's no problem tomorrow morning I'll go to meet them at Atitlán and Quetzaltenango. I'll borrow a camera to take with me.

Letter to Aunt Beatriz 22 July 1954
Dear Beatriz, [. . .]
It's all been great fun here, with shooting, bombing, speeches and other touches that have broken the monotony in which I was living. [. . .]

I leave in a few days (I don't know how many) for Mexico, where I am thinking of making a fortune by selling little whales to hang around the neck. [. . .]

Anyway I'll make sure I go the next time something breaks out, and I'm sure it will (if there is a next time), because the Yankees can't keep going without defending democracy somewhere or other. [. . .] Big hugs from your nephew-adventurer.

Letter to his mother 7 August 1954

Dear Mother,

[. . .]

There's nothing more to tell you about my life in Guatemala, as its rhythm is that of any Yankee colonial dictatorship. I've settled my affairs here and am hurrying away to Mexico. [. . .]

Letter to his parents August 1954

Dear Mother and Father,

[. . .]

I took refuge in the Argentine embassy, where they treated me very well, but I was not on the official list of those given asylum. Now the whole torment is over and I'm thinking of going on to Mexico sometime soon – but write to me here until further notice. [. . .]

You sent too much clothing, in my view, and spent too much on me; I'll be almost "flashy". But I don't think I deserve it (and there are certainly no signs that I'll change soon); not all the clothes will be useful because my big motto is little luggage, strong legs and the stomach of a fakir. Give my friendly greetings to the gang from Guatemala; I urge you to treat the guys who end up there as well as possible.

When all this calms down and things take on a new rhythm, I'll write to you in a more concise way. Hugs to you all from your first-born. I ask you to forgive me for the scares and to forget about me. What comes always falls from the skies. No one dies of hunger in America – nor in Europe, I guess.

Chau, Ernesto

Letter to Tita Infante Guatemala City, August 1954

Dear Tita,

I don't know when you will receive this letter, or even whether you will receive it, since now everything depends on the final destination of the bearer. This is why I won't give you any account of how things have gone here; my only aim was to introduce the bearer [. . .], a student of medicine who has chosen Argentina as his country for the duration of his exile from Guatemala. The bearer belonged to one of the bourgeois parties that cooperated loyally with Arbenz until his fall and concerned himself with the fate of the semi-exiled Argentines in these parts. For all these reasons I would like you to help this friend by giving him advice whenever necessary [. . .]; he will naturally be disoriented, as people are the first time they run around in the pampas.

I won't say anything about myself because it will be easy for me to write to you again before this introduction comes into your hands. In any case, let me say that I am continuing my voluntary exile and heading for Mexico, from where I'll make the great leap to Europe and, if possible, China.

Until it materializes somewhere in the world, here is an affectionate embrace by letter from your friend,

Ernesto

*

Atitlán is no better than the lakes in southern Argentina – far from it. Although it wasn't the day for making a final judgement, I dare to give one because the difference is very great. After I had seen the lake, I went to Chichicortenango and encountered some really interesting things in the life and rituals of the Indians. But I yielded and drank some rum and ate some trashy food, with the result that I had an attack of asthma. I was also frittering away too much money, so I came racing back to Guatemala City. The next day I picked up my passport and exit visa, and the day after that I collected the visa for Mexico. Today, Sunday, I have spent my time saying farewell to Guatemala, with a little outing to San Juan Sacatepéquez, a lot of passionate embraces and a little quickie. Tomorrow I'll take my leave of the people I want to say goodbye to, and on Tuesday morning I'll start the great Mexican adventure.

The first stage of the great adventure has turned out well and here I am installed in Mexico City,[50] though without knowing anything at all about what lies ahead. I left for the frontier bearing my slight misgivings. I had no trouble crossing the border, but the bribery professionals really got going on the Mexican side. I entered together with a good Guatemalan kid, an engineering student called Julio Roberto Cáceres Valle,[51] who also seems to have the travel bug. He's thinking of going for a while to Veracruz and trying the great leap from there. We did the trip to Mexico City together but now I am here alone – maybe he'll come back. The only really interesting thing during the journey was a side trip to the mines at Mitla, near Oaxaca. They are mines of the old Mixtec people, not very important by the look of them; they consist of a number of rectangular pits enclosed by four-sided structures adorned with rectilinear shapes. There are one or two constructions beneath the surface whose exact significance is not yet clear to me, although

50 He arrived in Mexico on 18 September 1954.
51 Known as "El Patojo" (the lame one) because of his short stature. He lived in Cuba after the victory of the revolution, then joined the liberation struggle in Guatemala and was killed in action. "Che", in *Episodes from the Revolutionary War* (New York 1996), draws a portrait of him in posthumous homage.

they must have been used by important persons as dressing rooms. It seems that the roofs were supported, in the main parts at least, by rounded, slightly conical pillars made of a kind of cement. All the structures are in stone held together by wood and gravel and have been touched up also with a kind of cement. There was not the imposing spectacle of Machu-Picchu, nor the beauty and fascination of Quiriguá, nor even the emotional power of the Salvadorean mines, but they did have things of interest and gave me a foretaste of what it will be like to see all the wonders here in Mexico. Today, or maybe tomorrow, I'll see U.P., given that Harold White isn't here and seems to have left for North America.

Days of feverish inefficiency have passed. I called on Petit,[52] and he took me out for a walk during which we discussed politics. He has a pleasant daughter, but she is being educated in the typical bourgeois-clerical way. Petit is obviously a deserter, who disguises this fact with quotations from the Pope and speaks of Catholic love as the only kind which can ever be solid, and so on. We visited the ruins of Teotihuacán, or something like that. There are huge pyramids without artistic value, and others that are of value. I'll go and see them again some time and note in detail what I saw – this time I only took a picture of Marta Petit with the new camera I have bought: a 35-exposure Zois 1 Kon 1:35.

Several days have passed blankly. After the very friendly discussion with Petit, I called just to leave my telephone number and he hasn't spoken to me again. I visited Helena; there's something odd between the two of them, but I'm not sure what. I also visited the museum of Mexican art, and although, as usual, I wasn't able to see it all, I did find interesting the displays of archaic culture, which contain some real works of art. I liked a Mayan and an Aztec head, and an obsidian vessel in the shape of a stylized monkey. There is also a very interesting monumental head with negroid features. Following them in interest, of course, are the paintings of the great quartet:

52 Ulises Petit de Murat, a scriptwriter and old friend of Ernesto's father.

Rivera, Tamayo, Siqueiros and Orozco. I was especially keen on Siqueiros, but they all seemed very fine – although the frescoes are in a very bad position for viewing.

Life in Mexico is in the throes of massive bureaucratization. Petit is now playing the fool in the biggest way. The latest developments are that Hilda is in Mexico at Tapachula (in what conditions, I don't know), and that I have been to see Dr Icharti, a young Peruvian who made a good impression, although I don't know if he'll be able to do anything for me. I have a photographer's job in the parks, so I'll see what comes of it. They are promising me a hundred and one things.

Several days have passed, and in general I can say that – apart from my disappointment at not being able to study anything other than medicine during the day – all my goals have worked out. On Monday I'll go and see about a medical job, and on Wednesday one of the others. Meanwhile I am continuing with my photography and meeting some people.

Francisco Petrone is by no means a Communist, but he is a sincere man and is convinced that his position is correct. He's not what you would call a cultured type, but on stage you can see that he immediately takes on the right role. I saw his directions and thought they were pretty good. The great idol Brown, on the other hand, was torn apart by the academics. Petit and I have already had some quarrels that point to a complete breakdown; at least he won't bug me any more. Hilda and I seem to have reached a status quo – we shall see.

I am still working discreetly with the photography, but you have to be fit and always on the go. I'm establishing myself at the hospitals and I think I will do something in that field, though not at the Institute of Nutrition. I've moved to a decent room in the city centre, for which I pay 100 pesos a month. It has a bathroom for both of us (El Patojo) and access to a kitchen. The landlady is a fat and ugly woman who looks as if she is quite a gossip.

The photography is not going badly, and the medicine promises to go not badly at all. The daily bread is obtained . . . Right now my intellectual life is non-existent, except for a little that I read at night and a few drops of daily study. I haven't yet been able to see the González Casanova couple and I don't know when I will. I see Hilda tomorrow.

A little water has passed under the bridge. In general things are like this: the photography is all I can really count on for my living, and it doesn't bring in enough. This week I had roughly 60 photos, which would have meant the same number of pesos (a not inconsiderable sum) if I had not been let down by a blurred roll of film. As for medicine, I put in three days at each of the hospitals, children's and general. At the general I am working on Pisani's food debasement, and at the children's they told me to present a plan of work (for which I already have an outline). Once I saw Icharti, the APRA doctor, and I have arranged to meet him again tomorrow. I can hardly speak about Mexico City, because I haven't got to know anything new.[53]

I haven't seen Petit, Petrone or Piaza for quite some time.

I still haven't met the people upstairs, even though my life is more organized and there would be no great problem in visiting them. The hospital keeps me tied up in the morning, although I don't do anything, and the evening alone is not enough for me to distribute the photos – so I am in deficit.

Letter to his mother

My dear Mother, (I confused you with the date)

[. . .]

Even Beatriz has decided to engage in reprisals, and the telegrams she used to send no longer arrive.

To tell you about my life is to repeat myself, because I am not doing anything new. The photography still gives me enough to live on and

53 See the letter that he sent to his family in November 1954.

I have no real hope of giving it up soon, even though I do research work every morning at two hospitals here. I think the best thing that could happen would be for me to get a little unofficial job as a country doctor near the capital; that would enable me to devote my time more easily to medicine for a few months. I am doing it because I was perfectly aware of how much I learned about allergy from Pisani. Just now I compared myself with people who studied in the United States and are no mugs in terms of orthodox knowledge, and I think that Pisani's method is streets ahead of all that and I want to become an expert in all the tricks of his system so that I can land on my feet somewhere. [. . .]

I have my work cut out now. I am busy every morning at the hospital, I spend my afternoons and Sundays taking pictures and evenings studying a little. I think I told you that I'm in a good apartment and make my own food, as well as having a bath every day thanks to the unlimited supply of hot water. As you see, I'm a new person in this respect, though in others I'm the same as before because I don't wash my clothes much and I still don't have enough money for a laundry.

The grant is a dream I have now abandoned; and I thought that in this huge country you had only to ask for something and it was done. You know that I have always been in favour of drastic decisions, and here they certainly pay off. Everyone loafs around but does not oppose what others do, so that I have the field open here or in the country area where I may go next. Of course, this is not making me lose sight of the fact that my objective is Europe, where I intend to go come what may. I haven't lost a bit of my contempt for the United States, but I would like to get to know New York at least. I'm not in the least bit afraid, because I know I'll leave just as anti-Yankee as when I arrived (if I do arrive).

I'm glad that people are waking up a bit, although I don't know what direction they are following. Anyway, the truth is that Argentina is extremely dull, even if the general picture as seen from here suggests that significant advances are being made and that there will be firm resistance to the crisis that the Yankees are about to unleash by dumping their food surpluses. [. . .]

The Communists do not have the same sense of friendship that you have, but it is as strong as or even stronger than yours. I have seen this quite clearly, and in the hecatomb that Guatemala became after the fall – where everyone expected only to fend for himself – the Communists kept their faith and comradeship alive and are the only group still working there.

I think they deserve respect, and sooner or later I will join the Party myself. What most prevents me from doing it right now is that I have a huge desire to travel in Europe, and I would not be able to do that if I was subject to rigid discipline.

So, Mother, until Paris

The gas is finished here and the old woman doesn't much want them to bring any more, so some of my paunch has been disappearing. Now we are also photographers for Agencia Latina,[54] but the first test worked out very badly when they planted me at the airport all afternoon to wait for some Argentine aviators and I lost the chance to take some pictures in the park (so that the day was a blank for me).

I haven't met any new people, except for some guys from the Honduran Revolutionary Democratic Party who seemed very right-wing. Helena defends them but there is no reason to do so; they are transforming the few things in them that are proletarian into something profoundly petty-bourgeois.

There is nothing new to report, now that everything is calmly following

54 The Latin News Agency, funded by the Argentine government.

its course. Piaza says that "maybe" he will get me a job selling at an OAS stand at the book fair, seeing that the photos don't earn me enough to live on. Otherwise, nothing new. I received news that the Guatemalan leftists are all under arrest, that Celia is getting married, and that Hercilia is marrying an old boy with money. I haven't met anyone interesting these days, and it seems that I never will if I keep this life up. It looks as if I'll have the bicycle in a few days from now.

Some things of a certain importance have happened during the last few days. In the street I met the boss of Agencia Latina,[55] a doctor, who took a liking to me and appointed me temporary correspondent. I got out the things from the Panamericana and they gave me a little money, not much; I think I'll be able to get by with it. The photography is coming along slowly. I am falling into debt, but I am also owed money. At the hospital I am working without any idea of where it will lead.

The days have passed with the usual chain of hopes and disappointments that characterize my proletarian life. The job at the book fair was a dream that is already over. Now I have a nicer job, though just as insecure: the boss of Agencia Latina has offered me about 500 pesos a month to work three times a week on a journalistic summary of events in Mexico.[56] For now I'm continuing with the photography, but earning less and less from it. A decision to do it on our own account is pending, but we do not have enough money.

The days succeed one another at breakneck speed. I am working a lot on allergies and am in close contact with the doctors.

In general I think I'll keep at it, although sharp shocks will go hand in hand with the victories. On Monday I take a test at the Agencia Latina to see if I can work there. I'm gradually abandoning the photography because

55 He is referring to Alfonso Pérez Vizcaino.
56 This was to cover the Panamerican Games, which took place in Mexico between 12 and 16 March 1955. Ernesto was an accredited Agencia Latina reporter from 31 January to 31 December 1955.

it tires me to travel all over the city for nothing. I'm working with my new salary of 700 pesos for only a few hours a day, but I'm still doing some photos and I got 150 pesos from the OAS for some pretty crude stuff. The criticism of Petit's work seems quite harsh, but I think I'll go to the function in a day or two to see how things are going.

My work at the hospital is going well, even though I am continually made aware that, with the exception of allergies, I don't know anything about medicine. I have two patients under treatment at each hospital. At the children's hospital my hands are tied and I am unable to do anything, while at the general I have my fill of liberty. I'm inclined to do an experiment in electrophoresis,[57] but I don't know what results it will give. On Sunday I went to the Virgin of Guadalupe Day, which wasn't as crowded as people say it usually is. As always, it was a mixture of pagan festivities and a bit of religion; a lot of Indians made up to look more like Indians, with a simple rhythmic music similar to that of Peru or Bolivia.

Letter to his mother

My dear Mother,

It's true, I've been quite lazy about writing, but the culprit, as always, has been Mister Money. The final part of the economically wretched year of 1954 – a part which treated me well – coincides with the end of my chronic hunger. I have an editing job at Agencia Latina for 700 pesos a month, which gives me enough to live on and has the additional advantage that it keeps me busy for only three hours three times a week. This allows me to spend the whole morning at the hospital, where I am making swellings with the Pisani method. [. . .]

I am still doing the photography, but also spending time on more important matters such as my "studies" and some odd little things that have come up here. There's not much money left over, but I hope

57 The motion of proteins (electrically charged molecules) in the presence of an electrical field.

to make 2,000 this December and, with a little help from fate, we'll do a bit of photography at the end of the coming year (at the beginning, I meant). Contrary to what you might think, I'm no worse than most photographers and the best in my group of friends – although in that group you need have only one eye to win the crown.

My immediate plan is to spend six months or so in Mexico (which I find interesting and like a lot), and during that time to apply in passing, as it were, for a visa to see "the children of the great power", as Arévalo calls them. If I get it I'll go there; if not, I'll see what more definite things turn up. Nor have I rejected the idea of seeing what is happening behind the Iron Curtain. As you see, nothing new since before.

As for scientific matters, I have a lot of enthusiasm and am profiting from this because it won't last. I am doing two research projects and may start on a third – all in connection with allergy – and although it goes very slowly I am collecting material for a little book that will appear (if ever) in a couple of years under the pretentious title "The Function of the Doctor in Latin America". I can speak as something of an authority on the subject, given that, although I don't know much medicine, I do have Latin America sized up. Of course, there is no more than a general plan of work and three or four chapters, but more than enough time.

As to the changes in my thinking which, as you see it, are becoming sharper, I assure you that they won't last long. There are two ways of arriving at what you so much fear: a positive way of direct persuasion, and a negative way of complete disenchantment. I arrived by the second way, but immediately convinced myself that it was necessary to continue by the first. The manner in which the gringos treat the American continent (remember that the gringos are Yankees) aroused my growing indignation, but at the same time

I studied the theoretical explanation for what they do and found that it was scientific. Then came Guatemala and all those things that are hard to relate; I saw how the whole object of someone's enthusiasm can weaken as a result of what those gentlemen decide, how a new balance sheet of red guilt and crime was being concocted, and how the Guatemalan traitors were themselves helping to spread all that in order to beg some scraps in the new order of things. I can't say, even approximately, at what moment I stopped reasoning and acquired something like faith, because the road was quite long and there was a lot of turning back. [. . .]

Letter to his mother 24 September 1955

Dear Mother,

This time my fears have come true, or so it seems, and the enemy you have hated for so many years has fallen. Here the reactions did not take long to appear: all the daily papers and foreign despatches jubilantly reported the fall of the murky dictator; the North Americans breathed with relief about the 425 million dollars they can now extract from Argentina; the bishop of Mexico City showed his satisfaction at Perón's downfall; and all the right-wing Catholics I have known in this country were also visibly content. But not my friends and I. We all followed with natural anxiety the fate of the Peronist government and the threats by the Navy to shell Buenos Aires. Perón fell as people of his ilk do fall, without the posthumous dignity of Vargas or the energetic denunciations of Arbenz, who called a spade a spade and named those guilty of aggression.

Here, progressives have described the Argentine denouement as "another victory for the dollar, the sword and the cross".

I know that today you will be overjoyed, that you will be breathing the air of freedom. [. . .]

Not long ago, I said in another letter to you that the military would not hand over power to civilians unless its caste domination was guaranteed. As things stand now, it will only hand over power to a government springing from the Democratic Party, or from one of the recently formed Social-Christian parties, which I imagine to be where [. . .] is active, that future member of the Chamber of Deputies and perhaps, eventually, leader of the yet to be founded Argentinist Party.

You will be able to say anywhere whatever it takes your fancy to say, with the absolute impunity that comes from being a member of the class in power, although I hope for your sake that you are the black sheep in the flock. I confess to you quite frankly that Perón's fall has greatly embittered me, not on his account but because of what it means for the Americas. For however much you hate the idea, and however much it has been forced to give way in the recent period, Argentina was the champion of all of us who think that the enemy is in the north. To me, who lived through Guatemala's bitter hours, what happened in Argentina was a copy at a distance; and when I saw that, together with the loyal news (odd to call it that), the voice of Córdoba was to be heard – a city theoretically occupied – I began to lose any clear picture of the situation. Afterwards everything happened in exactly the same way: the president resigned, a junta began to negotiate from a position of resistance and then collapsed, a military man came to the fore with a little naval officer by his side (the only detail added since Guatemala); then Cardinal Copello proudly spoke to the nation, calculating how his business would prosper under the new regime; the whole of the world's press – on this side of the world – launched its utterly familiar yells; the junta refused to give Perón a passport but declared freedom for one and all. People such as yourself will think you can see the

93

dawning of a new day; I assure you that Frondizi no longer sees it, since in the event that the Radicals come out on top it won't be he who achieves it but, with the blessing of the military, Yadarola, Santander or someone else serving the interests of the Yankees and the clergy. Perhaps at first you won't see the violence, because it will be exercised in a circle far from your own. [. . .]

In time the Communist Party will be put out of circulation, and perhaps a day will come when even Papa feels that he made a mistake. Who knows what will meanwhile have become of your wandering son. Perhaps he will have decided to set up shop in his native country (the only one possible), or to begin a life of real struggle. [. . .]

Perhaps one of the bullets so common in the Caribbean will put an end to my days (this is neither idle talk nor a concrete possibility: it's just that a lot of bullets fly around in these parts). Perhaps I'll simply keep wandering long enough to complete a solid education and to take the pleasures I have awarded myself for this life, before seriously devoting myself to the pursuit of my ideal. Things develop with tremendous speed, and no one can predict where they will be next year and why.

I don't know if you got the formal announcement of my marriage and the arrival of an heir – from Beatriz's letter it would seem not. In that case, I officially inform you of it, so that you can tell other people the news; I am married to Hilda Gadea and we will soon be having a child. I received the papers from Beatriz; they interest me a lot. I would like some correspondence about the events of the last few days, and above all a weekly copy of *Nuestra Palabra*.[58]

Chau

Kisses to all the family, and greetings from Hilda.

*

58 The official paper of the Argentine Communist Party.

The last days of the year are approaching and it looks as if some economic change is shaping up. I keep on with my scientific research, working on digested food and preparing to work on blood electrophoresis and Urbach equipment. At the children's hospital, they want me to do some paid experimental work. I am still working at Agencia Latina, though I haven't been paid anything yet. My studies are at a standstill: I read very little medicine and a little more literature, but I hardly ever write anything. As to public relations, they are more or less the same as before; I haven't made any really worthwhile friendship, either intellectual or sexual. I'll spend Christmas Eve snugly in my sleeping bag, keeping night watch over a stand of toys. I've left off the photography and there are moments when I regret this, for I'm not being paid anything and that always earned me a little. Still, now I have time to spend on other things and in the New Year I'll discipline myself a bit more. On the educational side I feel like a grandfather, now that El Patojo, in response to my advice about his life, has decided to go back and help his mother in Guatemala.

At a political level, it is worth noting the change in the fortunes of Don Edelberto Torres and his son, the one released and expelled, the other a fugitive.

Nothing new to be noted here, except the oldness of another year that is finished. As always, Hilda got angry because I didn't want to go with her to a party; I spent New Year's Eve on watch at the OAS building. There's nothing new to relate. They haven't paid me at Agencia Latina, and maybe they won't pay me for a while longer because the dough is coming, or rather isn't coming, all the way from Buenos Aires.

Today I feel a bit like the grandfather who gives wise advice; El Patojo has left for Guatemala with a "jerk" of a brother. This comes from a conversation in which I told him he was running away from something and not fighting (as he had claimed in a letter to his mother that he read to me); the next day he decided to leave, and a little later the brother was accompanying him.

Apart from the dough I had lent him before, I gave him 150 pesos more that Piaza lent me. I'm in a strange situation: I'm counting on my pay from Agencia Latina, but they feed me with promises and never say anything more specific. I have great hopes in the scientific field, although they are not yet justified by the reality. I have begun studying how to do the electrophoresis with filter paper, and I hope to begin working on it in a week or two. I don't write home much, so I don't know a lot from there.

I now have my first month's pay and have already spent it – not to mention the things I haven't paid but owe. I'm not too worried about this, for the following reason. With Dr Cortés I am looking after a patient who pays me 20 pesos per consultation, four times a day, and with this I'll have enough to eat until the next remittance from Agencia Latina. I'm on good terms with the agency, despite the fact that Dr Pérez has got me taped; so I'm trying to persuade him, in a jokey sort of way, to send me to José Figueres's place in Costa Rica. I haven't any news from "El Patojo", nor from home. There's just a Peruvian student who has written asking what I think will happen in Guatemala. The scientific work is held up for a while because of my unstable situation; I have to get out of the house and don't know where to go.

The housing problem is still unresolved, and I'm practically living on air in every sense. The homespun electrophoresis machine works slowly, while the other work is virtually at a standstill. With Dr Cortés I am looking after a patient who will, I think, get a lot better; I charge her 20 pesos a consultation. I hope the coming week will be an eventful one.

[. . .]

My patient seemed much worse. I did some more tests and she turned out to be sensitive to a number of foods, so I have taken her off them. Despite everything I still haven't been paid, and there's no way of making ends meet. What bothers me most is that Agencia Latina does not pay as promptly as it should. As for the big projects, there's nothing new. Tomorrow I'll finish the article on Guatemala they asked me for and then spend the whole week writing letters, as I'm very behind with my correspondence.

Days of uncertainty, with everything up in the air. I got my pay for January and have already spent it (it's late February now). Now that the Panamerican Games are coming, I'll have to work like a slave and put the stuff at the hospital to one side. My patient is stable, exactly where I left her. I think I have broken with Hilda for good after a melodramatic scene. I've started to fancy a girl who's a chemist: she's not very intelligent and doesn't know a lot, but she has a very appealing freshness and fantastic eyes. I'll present a piece of work to the Allergy Congress in April on cutaneous tests with digested food.

More than a month has gone by since my last diary entry. A lot of things have happened, or not such a lot – it depends on your point of view. The Panamerican Games caused me a hell of a lot of trouble, and when it seemed there would be no compensation a promise came through that I would get some. Almost at the same time, however, I heard that Agencia Latina was being inexplicably wound up, with the resulting worries about money. Now it seems they will pay me the two months they owe, plus three months' redundancy and 2,000 pesos for the photos. That means something like 5,000 pesos in all, which would come in very handy and allow me to pay off some debts, travel around Mexico and then clear the hell out.

The work cost me some troubles, but at the same time I made two good friends: Fernando Margolles and Severino Rossell, "El Guajiro".[59] I'm living in a new place and, as usual, already have problems paying the rent.

[. . .] Scientifically, I'm committed to finishing a piece of work for the Allergy Congress and I think I'll do it. They have invited me to go to Nuevo Laredo, near the frontier with the gringos, but it would be to work there for two years and I'm not prepared to do it for that long. My plans are simpler: until March I'll do the allergy work and present the paper; in May, June

59 That is: the peasant.

97

and July I'll travel round Mexico from north to south and east to west; in July-August I'll head for Veracruz and wait for a boat to take me to Cuba or Europe – if that's not on, I'll be in Caracas by December. We'll see how it works out.

A lot of water has passed under my bridge; now [. . .] I've turned up as an intern at the hospital. This is how things developed. I went to León, Guanajuato, and presented my paper: 'Cutaneous Investigations with Semi-Digested Food Antigens.'[60] The paper went down reasonably well, and Salazar Mallén, head of the allergy branch in Mexico, made some comments on it. It will now be published in the journal *Alergia*. Salazar Mallén promised me some financial assistance for research work and a position as intern at the general hospital, but that remains to be seen.

There's no definite news about the cash from Agencia Latina. Something else worth noting is that I have got myself on the Mexican electoral register, thanks to the complete absence of checks. You just show up, give a name and address, and that's it. That's what the elections will be like.

At Guanajuato I saw the celebrated short farces based on Cervantes. They were performed by local amateur players, in a natural setting with a church as backdrop. Most of the actors lacked class, but the setting was so natural that all of that went unnoticed.

After many adventures I am now established at the general hospital and working quite hard, although in a somewhat disorderly fashion. The food is rather bad for me: if I eat it I get asthma; if I don't I go hungry. Salazar Mallén pays me 150 pesos [. . .]. Agencia Latina says it will pay up and that would mean 5,000 pesos – we'll see if it's true. I now spend my time getting to know the area surrounding Mexico City, together with Hilda. We've been to see some magnificent Rivera frescoes at an agricultural college, and also visited Puebla.

60 A paper presented at the Ninth National Congress of Allergists, held at the León School of Medicine, Guanajuato, 25-30 April 1955. The paper was later published in the *Revista Iboamericana de Alergología*, Mexico City, May 1955, p. 157.

Some good and some bad things have been happening. I'm still not sure what my future will be like. Agencia Latina has paid up, but not all of it, and I'll only have 2,000 pesos left to pay some bills and buy some presents. They invited me to the Youth Festival but I would have had to pay my own way; and as I was still counting on getting the money I announced to all and sundry that I was planning to go to Spain on 8 July. Now it's all come to nothing and I'm going ahead with my plan to travel round Mexico from 1 September on. As a sporting event, I should mention the ascent of the lower side of Popocatepetl by an ad hoc group of valiant mountaineers (which included myself). It is wonderful and I would like to do it again fairly often. Pascual Lozano, the Venezuelan, fell behind a little before catching up, even though we took him in tow for the final stage. Another event has been the revolution in Argentina, which fills me with unease because my brother is in the marines. The funny event was my invitation to take Hilda and a Peruvian friend to a football match. It got off to a splendid start with lighted mothballs and ended with buckets of shit, which all three of us got.

A political event was that I met Fidel Castro, the Cuban revolutionary. He is a young, intelligent guy, very sure of himself and extraordinarily audacious; I think we hit it off well.[61]

A sporting event was our unsuccessful climbing of "Popo", when we stopped a few metres from the top because Margolles had frozen feet and was scared to go on.

A tourist event was Margolles's departure for the US.

A scientific event was the appearance of my first solo publication in medicine, in the journal *Alergia*: 'Investigaciones cutáneas con antigenos alimentarios semidigeridos'; passable.

In physiology I've become a cat surgeon.

Months have gone by. I'm married to Hilda; we've moved and everything

61 This meeting took place towards the end of July 1955 in Mexico City.

seems to be shaping up for some agreeable months contemplating the future.[62]

Politically important have been the inglorious fall of Perón and the seizure of power by a military clique with links to the clergy and the centre parties. I have kept my studies a little more compact; I only read about allergy and am studying some English and a little algebra. My work covers only three themes, with one for the future. They are: histamines in the blood, histamine in the lung tissue of tuberculars, and progesterone; I am thinking of doing some serum electrophoresis. On another point, I have bought a camera to replace the one they stole from me, and I am learning to touch-type. I still don't know if I'm going to work at the United Nations; the idea repels but the money attracts.

There's not a lot to add, except that I have finally reached the top of Popo. It was an easy climb, almost without problems, and we reached the lower slope at 6.30 (we didn't go any higher). But I couldn't take any proper photos because everything was covered in mist. I'm thinking of going soon to Yucatán to get to know the whole Mayan region. There's no political news, except for my family's heated letters that lay into me for supporting Perón against the liberators.[63]

I went to a meeting where views were exchanged about the fall of Perón; the reporter was a Señor Orfila, and I later found out that much of his fury against Perón was due to quarrels that he, Perón, had had with the Fondo de Cultura Económica (of which he was director).[64] Things went well until late in the meeting, when they laid into the comrades and I jumped up to give the gentleman a piece of my mind. But I was pretty upset and couldn't coordinate what I was saying; in the end I proposed that the sending of a congratulatory note should be left until the government had achieved

62 They married at Tepoztlán on 18 August 1955.
63 See the letter to his mother dated September 1955.
64 After the victory of the Cuban Revolution, Orfila maintained close relations with "Che" and always expressed his solidarity with Cuba.

something definite in areas such as trade union democracy and the running of the economy. But Orfila asserted that they couldn't pay attention to "such matters as exchange controls which were up to a point secondary". The Socialists are heading up shit creek.

I have done my much-awaited farewell trip around the south-east of Mexico and managed to cover at least superficially the Mayan region. We went to Veracruz by train – a completely uninteresting journey. Veracruz is a small and not very lively port, with all the features of a little town of Spanish descent. The beaches are small, clean and level; the sea warm.

We came across an Argentine ship there, *El Granadero*, and I got them to give me a few kilos of *mate*. Boca del Río is a small fishing town some ten kilometres to the south of Veracruz. I went there to watch a day's fishing on Rosendo Rosado's boat *La Tonina*; the life and the problems of the fishing community are very interesting.

After five days in Veracruz, we took a bus heading south. We spent the first night at Lake Catemaco, but we couldn't visit it because it was a rainy day. Then we pushed on and spent a night at Coatzacoalcos (a fairly important sea port), by the side of the river of the same name. I arrived with asthma. The next day we crossed the river. The other side is called Allende, and from there we took a train and reached Palenque in the evening; we went by jeep from the station to the hotel.

The ruins of Palenque are magnificent. The old population centre lies on the side of a hill, from which an area four by six kilometres stretches out into the forest. It has still not been explored, even though a clear picture exists of the built-up area hemmed in by thick vegetation.

The neglect shown by the authorities is almost complete. It took four years to clean the main tomb, one of the most valuable archaeological jewels in the Americas, whereas the right team of workers could have done it in three months. The most important structures are: the palace, which has a series of galleries and patios with stone carvings and stucco arrises of high artistic quality. The Temple of Inscriptions, also called the Tomb Temple, has a tomb unique in the Americas which is entered from the upper part of the pyramid; a long tunnel with a trapezoidal roof then leads down to a broad chamber in which you find a stone monolith 3.80 metres long by 2.20 wide and 0.27 thick, adorned with hieroglyphs representing the sun, the moon and the planet Venus.

Beneath the tablet is a fully carved catafalque that used to hold the corpse of a prominent figure.

There were jewels of different sizes, all of them jade. Worthy of mention at Palenque are the beauty and delicacy of its stucco bas-reliefs, executed with an art that is subsequently lost as the power of the Third Empire comes to assert itself, where one mainly notices a Toltec influence that is more monumental but much less sculptural.

The sculptural motifs at Palenque are more human than those of the Aztecs or Toltecs. Mostly you see full-length human shapes set amid historical events or rituals, together with the most important gods in their Olympus: the sun, the moon, Venus, water, and so on.

According to the classification made by the North American archaeologist Morley, Palenque was a category-two population centre within the Mayan area. (He gives category-one status only to Copán, Tikal, Uxmal and Chichén-Itzá.) Archaeological investigations have shown that Palenque erected monuments during the first quarter of Baktún 9 (AD 435-534), more or less contemporaneous with those at Piedras Negras, the other artistic centre of the empire. Both flourished under the First Empire. In all there are 19 cities in Morley's category two, although the most recent investigations tend to give greater importance to Palenque. Category one or not, almost everyone thinks that it is definitely the Mayan town where stucco work of the finest art and technique was executed.

We left Palenque in the evening and took a train south-east to the small port of Campeche, where we spent a day. There is not a lot to see there –

only the ruins of forts built as a defence against pirates. Two hours by bus took us to Mérida, a fairly large town for its type but with a very provincial life. Mérida is not a sea port, and all its features are of a town 500 (not just 30) kilometres from the sea. It gets quite cool at night considering how hot it is there. The town museum is very badly presented and supplied, but it does have some interesting things. The main attractions of Mérida are the ruined Mayan cities in the vicinity, of which we visited two of the most important: Uxmal and Chichén-Itzá.[65]

According to the tradition of Chilam-Balam of Chumayel, Chichén-Itzá was discovered and populated by the Mayans as they expanded in the fourth century or thereabouts, although the first date that can be read with any certainty corresponds to AD 878. It was the time when the abandonment of the cities of the old empire was being completed, and work on Chichén-Itzá was started within the framework of the new empire. The Itzen had withdrawn from the city in 692 and settled in the Campeche region. Later the Mayan renaissance, roughly spanning two centuries from 997 to 1194, saw the rise of the Mayapán League and the building of the monuments we see today, with their Chac-Mool and plumed serpents, although the foundations on which they were built belong to the earlier Mayan period. The resurgence seems to have been due to the Quetzalcoatl invasion from the central plain of Mexico, which brought with it the Eagle and the Serpent that are the basic emblem of that region. The decline of Chichén-Itzá began when it lost the civil war with Mayapán – these two, plus Uxmal, having made up the governing trio of the Mayan confederation. Mayapán called on Mexican mercenaries for support, destroyed the power of its opponents, and carried them off to live in its midst. Then in 1441 any kind of centralized government seems to have come to an end in the north of Yucatan, as civil war broke the hegemony of the Mayapán House of Cocomina.

Let us begin a description of its temples and other structures. The first is

65 The photo of the ruins of Chichén-Itzá was taken by "Che" on his trip and has not been published before. That of Uxmal was taken by his son, Ernesto.

the Cave of Sacrifices, situated in the north of the city and nowadays filled with greenish water. On its south side it has a small altar from which the victims were probably cast down together with the ceremonial objects. Although a lot has already been extracted from the waters, the amount of jewellery still preserved there must be quite fantastic. The cave has a diameter of 40-60 metres, a height of 10 metres and a depth of 20 metres. There is another one on the south side, called Xtoloc, from which drinking water used to be drawn – but in this case the approach is along a gently sloping ramp that goes right down to the water's edge. The so-called Castle, the city's great pyramid, is more than 500 metres to the south, with a main bridge overlooking the cave to which it is joined by a six-metre-wide causeway raised five metres above the ground. The Castle is possibly the oldest of the temples still standing; it has 91 steps on each side (giving a total of 364), which are thought by some to represent the days of the year, and a final one situated above makes up the total. Crowning the structure is a not very well finished temple with few carvings, but in a tomb that one passes going down a slab-covered stone ramp there are sculptures and jewels of great archaeological value. At the bottom, a door leads along an underground stairway to the chamber containing what Morley considered the greatest archaeological treasure in the Americas (though in my view that is an exaggeration): namely, a life-sized red jaguar encrusted with 43 apple-green jade discs imitating the jaguar's spots. A hundred or so metres to the east lies the Temple of the Warriors, the most majestic and evocative of the structures at Chichén-Itzá, which is crowned with a series of colonnades featuring the plumed serpent and Chac-Mool; the later is a reclining figure of great dignity, which holds its feet close to the buttocks and supports an offering plate.

Alongside the Temple of the Warriors is the series of columns for which the place has been baptised The Thousand Columns, and then a number of heavily damaged structures in which one finds two or three pelota courts and a steam bath. The Main Pelota Court, measuring 146 metres by 36, lies a couple of hundred metres west of the Castle. Still embedded in the wall are the two stone hoops through which the solid rubber balls had to be thrown, not with the hand but with elbows or knees, and tradition has it that this was so difficult that anyone who managed it had the right to remove all the jewellery from those present. On the east side of the Pelota Court is the Temple of the Jaguars, with some frescoes in very poor condition. Facing the north side of the Castle are a number of small platforms of no great architectural interest; they are called The Pines, House of the Eagles, Tzompantli (place of the skulls, where the heads of the sacrificial victims were kept). Further to the south, along the present-day road to Mérida, one finds what Morley calls the "Tomb of the High Priest" and Mexican anthropologists "The Ossuary"; it contains a large number of offerings and is one of the few places where pearls have been found (in the new tomb at Palenque there is one that resembles a tear). Today there remain only two large heads of plumed serpents and some rectangular columns. Next come a number of minor temples, such as the Stag Temple and the Temple of Chac-Mool, formerly called the Red House, and eventually one reaches the Spiral or the Observatory, one of the principal structures in size and significance. The Spiral is the observatory where the Mayans used to conduct their astronomical research; its two huge platforms support a (now partly ruined) tower twelve metres high that one climbs by a narrow spiral staircase, and the rays of the sun and moon and the spring and autumn equinoxes are able to pass through an opening in the tower. At the southernmost point of Chichén-Itzá lies Las Monjas (The Nuns), a fairly ramshackle structure with fine guard-shaped decorations and some fresco remnants. To the east is an unpretentious structure, Akab'Dzib, which also has some small remnants of frescoes.

Uxmal is a much later city than Chichén-Itzá, having been founded in the tenth century by a Mexican chief of the Xiu family, Ah Zuitok Tutl Xiu.

Uxmal remained neutral in the wars between Chichén and Mayapán and later helped to overthrow the Mayapán chief in 1441, although Uxmal itself had already been abandoned. It is a really beautiful city, much softer than Chichén, though not in the same artistic league as Palenque. It is a pity that it has not been as well studied and reconstructed as Chichén, for it has structures of great beauty such as the Governor's Palace, which has been classified as the finest in the Mayan region, although personally I like the Quadrangle at Las Monjas more. The Governor's Palace, which is 95 metres long by 12 metres wide and 8 metres high, was executed with great refinement. The plumed serpent and other Aztec motifs are not seen much at Uxmal, but in my view the whole mosaic of its friezes is very similar to the Zapotec or Miltec work in the region of Mitla-Oaxaca. In a northern corner of the Governor's House lies the so-called Temple of the Tortoises, a little archaeological jewel. The Quadrangle of Las Monjas is a yard 80 by 65 metres enclosed by four wings; you enter it through a wide trapezoidal domed gate on the southern side, and facing you are the architecturally very beautiful Temple of Venus (a modern appellation) and the exquisitely executed east and west wings. Beside this structure rises the so-called Temple of the Seer, which was probably the city's most important ceremonial building. These are the most significant and the best preserved structures, but there are quite a lot of others such as the North and North-East Group, the Terrace of the Monuments, the Pelota Court, the Cemetery, the West Group, the Dovecote, the Great Pyramid, the South Group, the Pyramid of the Old Woman, which have not yet been fully cleaned and restored.

The next day (or rather, that same evening) we set off for Veracruz on board the *Ana Graciela*, a little motor vessel of 150 tons. The first day went well, but on the second a real northerly wind blew up and had us reeling all over the place. We rested a day in Veracruz and then headed for Mexico City on the road that goes via Córdova; we stopped off there for an hour to look around. It's no great shakes but is still a very pleasant town, more than

800 metres above sea level, with cool air in a tropical setting and a lot of coffee fields. The nearby town of Orizaba is already much more like the Andes, and so gloomier and colder. The River Blanco lies just outside, as if an extension of the town; it was the site of an historic massacre of workers protesting against exploitation by a Yankee company – I don't remember in which year.

Only two important events. One of them shows that I am getting old: a girl whom I helped to write a thesis mentioned me as one of those who gave her guidance (it's the custom here to dedicate your thesis to half the world) and I felt rather pleased. The other was a very nice experience. I went to Iztacihualt, the third largest volcano in Mexico; it was a very long way, and the novelty was that some people were travelling by horse. At first I managed to keep up with the best, but at a certain point I stopped for five minutes to treat a blister and when I got going again I raced to catch up with the rest of the column. I did catch up, but I was already feeling sore and in the end I began to feel tired. Then I had the luck to meet a girl who couldn't move any more, and on the pretext of helping her (she was on horseback) I went along dangling from the stirrup. We eventually reached the tent where we were to spend the night, which in my case I spent chilled to the bone and sleeping badly. When we arrived the ground was dry, but when we got up the next day there were 30 or 40 centimetres of snow and it was still falling. It was decided to keep going anyway, but we couldn't even reach the neck of the volcano and at 11.00 we started on our way back.

The whole road had been dusty and stony on the way up, but now it was covered with snow. I, who suffer from poor circulation in my feet, was wearing five pairs of socks, so that I was barely able to walk. But a muleteer with a loaded mule passed by as cool as a cucumber, his feet in the air, giving me all sorts of complexes about myself. It was when we came to the wooded area that the scenery became most attractive, for the snow in the pines was quite magnificent and the beauty was enhanced by the still falling snow. I was exhausted by the time I reached home.

Once more to Iztacihualt, after a number of failures. This time it was like this: nine of us arrived at the foot of the slope as it was getting light and began to climb up along the edge of La Gubia in the direction of the Ago shelter, desperate to straighten our knees. When we attacked the snow, two turned back. I remained in the last group and the guy accompanying me turned back when we attacked the glacier and saw it was pure ice, so that I remained alone and moved ahead until I fell down clutching a shoulder in the ice. The fall made me more cautious and I went on very slowly. The guide tried to encourage me by showing me how to climb up, but then he came crashing down. He passed alongside me like a ball, desperately trying to drive his axe into the ice, and after some 80 metres he did finally come to a stop near a precipice from which there was a great leap into the shit. After the guide's big crash, we all descended very carefully and realized that it takes longer to go down than to go up. The guide felt exhausted and wandered away from the downward path, so that it was 6.00 by the time we reached the foot of the slope.

A lot of time has gone by and a lot of things have happened. I'll just note down the most important. Since 15 February 1956 I am a father: Hilda Beatriz Guevara is my first-born. I belong to the Roca del CE group of Mexico. Five job offers fell through and I started work as a cameraman for a small company; I have been making rapid advances in cinematography. My plans for the future are pretty vague, but I hope to finish a couple of research projects. This may be an important year for my future. I've given up hospitals. I'll write about it in greater detail.

Letter to his mother Mexico City, 15 July 1956[66]

[Mother: I have received your letter. It sounds as if you were going

66 A copy of the original is in "Che"'s Personal Archives; a few corrections and amplifications have been added in square brackets.

through a pretty bad depression. It contains much wisdom and many things I didn't know about you.]

I am not Christ or a philanthropist, Mother; I'm the complete opposite of Christ, and philanthropy doesn't seem to me [. . .].[67] I fight for the things in which I believe, with the weapons in my reach, and I try to leave the other lying flat instead of letting myself be nailed to a cross or whatever. As to the hunger strike, you are quite wrong. We started two: on the first occasion, they released 21 of the 24 they were holding; on the second, they announced that they would release Fidel Castro tomorrow, the head of the Movement. If this happens as they said, there would be just two of us left behind bars. I don't want you to think, as Hilda suggests, that the two of us left have been sacrificed; we are simply the two whose papers are in [bad] order, so we cannot avail ourselves of the resources that our comrades have used. My plans are to leave for the closest country that will give me asylum – not so easy, given the inter-American reputation they have stuck on me – and from there to be prepared for whenever my services are necessary. I'll say again that I won't be able to write for a fairly long time.

What [really] gets me down is your lack of understanding for all this and your advice about moderation, egoism, and so on: in other words, the most execrable qualities an individual can have. Not only am I not moderate now, I shall try never to be. And if I ever detect in myself that the sacred flame has given way to a timid votive flicker, the least I can then do is vomit over my own shit. As to your appeal for moderate egoism, that is, for common lily-livered individualism (the qualities of XX.), I must tell you that I have done a lot to wipe him out – I mean, not exactly that unfamiliar spineless type, but the other bohemian type, unconcerned about his neighbour and imbued

67 Word illegible.

with a sense of self-sufficiency deriving from an awareness (mistaken or not) of my own strength. During these prison days and the period of training that preceded them, I have identified totally with my comrades in the cause. I remember a phrase that once seemed to me idiotic or at least bizarre, referring to such a total identification among the members of a fighting body that the very concept of the "I" disappeared and gave way to the concept of the "we". It was a Communist morality and may, of course, appear to be a doctrinaire exaggeration, but in reality it was (and is) a beautiful thing to be able to feel that stirring of "we".

(The stains are not tears of blood but tomato juice.)

You are profoundly mistaken in believing that great inventions or works of art arise out of moderation or "moderate egoism". Any great work requires passion, and the revolution requires passion and audacity in large doses – things that humanity as a whole does have. Another odd thing is your repeated mention of God the Father; I hope you are not returning to the fold of your youth. I should also warn you that the series of SOSs are a waste of time: Petit got the wind up, while Lezica dodged the issue and gave Hilda (who went there against against my orders) a sermon on the obligations of political asylum. Raúl Lynch behaved well, from a distance, and Pavilla Nervo said that they were different ministries. They could all help, but on condition that I renounce my ideals. I don't think that you would prefer a son who is alive but a Barabbas to one who died somewhere fulfilling what he took to be his duty. The [attempts to give] assistance do no more than cause trouble for them and for myself.

[But you have some clever ideas (at least to my way of thinking), and the best of them is the business of the interplanetary rocket – a word I would like.] Moreover, it is true that, after I have set wrongs [right] in

Cuba, I'll go somewhere else; and it is also true that I'd be really done for if I were shut up in some bureaucratic office or allergy clinic. When all is said and done, though, it seems to me that this pain – the pain of a mother entering old age who wants her son alive – is a feeling that should be respected, a feeling that I have a duty to heed and actually want to heed. I would like to see you, not only to comfort you but to comfort myself for my sporadic and unconfessable yearnings.

Mother, I kiss you and promise to be with you if there is nothing new. Your son,

el Che

Letter to his mother Mexico City, 15 [probably November 1956]
Dear Mother,
Still here in Mexico, I am answering your last letters. I can't give you much news about my life, because I am only doing a little gymnastics and reading a huge amount (especially the things you can imagine). I see Hilda some weekends.

I've given up trying to get my case resolved through legal channels, so my residence in Mexico will be only temporary. In any event, Hilda is going with the little girl to spend New Year with her family. She'll be there for a month, then we'll see what happens. My long-term aim is to see something of Europe, if possible to live there, but that is getting more and more difficult. With the kind of illness I have, it seems to keep getting worse and is shaken off only in the grave.

I had a project for my life which involved ten years of wandering, then some years of medical studies and, if any time was left, the great adventure of physics.

Now that is all over. The only clear thing is that the ten years of wandering look like being more (unless unforeseen circumstances put an end to all wandering), but it will be very different from the kind I imagined. Now, when I get to a new country, it won't be to look around and visit museums or ruins, but also (because that still interests me) to join the people's struggle.

I have read the latest news from Argentina about the refusal to grant legal status to three new parties and the left-overs of what the CP used to have. Unexpected as it is, this measure is less symptomatic than everything that has been happening for some time in Argentina. All its actions display such a clear tendency – to favour one caste or class – that there can be no mistake or confusion. That class is the national landowning class, allied, as always, with foreign investors.

If I say these rather sharp things to you, it is a case of "bashing you because I love you". Now comes a hug, one of my last from Mexico. And since I am issuing admonitions, here is a final one: the mother of the Maceos complained of no longer having any sons to offer to Cuba. I won't ask so much of you – only that my price, or the price of seeing me, should not be something that is against your convictions or that might make you regret it one day.

Chau

Letter to his mother

Dear Mother,[68]

I write from somewhere in Mexico, where I am waiting for things to be sorted out. The air of freedom is in fact the air of clandestinity, but no matter: it adds an interesting touch of mystery.

My health is very good and my optimism even better. As to your judgements about the liberators, I see that little by little, almost without wishing it, you are losing confidence in them.

[What you said about trust and a firm objection is one of the most tragic things you wrote, but don't worry, I won't show it to anyone.

68 This letter probably dates from August or September 1956, after Ernesto's release.

Just imagine what the Egyptian newspapers are saying, for example, and the "West's loss of trust". It is logical that they have much more trust in a fiefdom belonging to them than in a real country, even if it doesn't have a project of independence.] The oil won't be Argentine either. The bases that they so much feared Perón would provide will be provided by them; or at least they will grant a similar concession. Freedom of expression is already a myth: we used to have a Peronist myth, now we have a myth of liberation. [. . .] By the time of the general elections they will have banned the Communist Party and will be trying every means of neutralizing Frondizi, who is the best that Argentina can hope for. In the end, Mother, the prospect I see from here is one of desolation for the movement of the Argentine poor: that is, for the majority of the population.

Well, I have little time to write and I don't want to waste it on such matters. In fact, though, I don't have much to tell you about my own life, as I spend it doing exercises and reading. I think I'll emerge from all this very strong in economics, although I have forgotten to take my pulse and to auscultate myself (I never did that well). My way seems to be slowly but surely diverging from that of clinical medicine, but it never diverges so far that I do not have some nostalgia for the hospital. What I told you about the professorship in physiology was a lie, but not much of one. It was a lie because I never thought of accepting it, but there was such an offer and it was very likely that they would have given it to me, since there was an interview appointment and so on. Anyway, that's all history now. Saint Karl has acquired a new recruit.

I can't say anything of the future. Write and tell me of family things, which are very refreshing in these latitudes.

Mother, a big hug from

your *clandestine* son

Letter to his mother (approximately October 1956)

Dear Mama,

Your prickly son, a mean one at that, is not a good-for-nothing; he is like Paul Muni was when he said what he said in that voice full of pathos and moved off amid darkening shadows and specially composed music.[69] My current occupation means I am always on the go, here today, there tomorrow – which is why I haven't been to see my relatives. (I confess that, as far as tastes go, I would probably have more in common with a whale than with a bourgeois married couple employed at worthy institutions that I would wipe from the face of the earth if it was given to me to do so. I don't want you to think that this is a simple aversion on my part; it is a basic distrust. Lezica has shown that we speak different languages and have no points of contact.) I have given you this explanation in brackets because, after what I wrote, I thought you would imagine that I was in the process of becoming a bourgeois; so, being too lazy to start again and remove the paragraph, I embarked on a lengthy explanation that strikes me as rather unconvincing. Full stop, new paragraph.

In a month's time Hilda will go to visit her family in Peru, profiting from the fact that she is no longer a political criminal but a some-what misguided representative of the worthy anti-Communist party, the APRA. I am in the process of changing the order of priorities in my studies. Previously I devoted myself for better or worse to medicine, and spent my spare time informally studying Saint Karl. The new stage in my life requires me to change the order: now Saint Karl comes first; he is the axis and will remain so for however many years the spheroid has room for me on its outer mantle; medicine is a more or less trivial diversion, except for one small area on which

69 The reference is to the film *I Am a Fugitive from a Chain Gang*, in which Paul Muni played the leading role.

I am thinking of writing more than one substantive study – the kind that makes the bookshop cellars tremble beneath its weight. As you will remember – and if you don't, I'll remind you – I was set on editing a book on the function of the doctor, and so on. Well, I only managed to finish a couple of chapters, which smack of a *Bodies and Souls*-type of newspaper serial – just badly written and displaying at every step complete ignorance of the real heart of the matter; and so I decided to study. Moreover, I had to come up with a number of conclusions and therefore set aside my essentially adventurist approach. I decided first to carry out the main tasks, to rush at the order of things with a shield on my arm (a complete fantasy), and then, if the windmills did not break my nut, to sit down and write.

I owe Celia the letter of praise that I will write after this if I have enough time. The others are in debt to me because I have the last word with everyone, even with Beatriz. Tell her that the papers are getting through fine and giving me a very good picture of all the wonderful deeds of the government. I have carefully cut things out from them, following the example set by my pater, and Hilda has undertaken to follow the example set by her mater. A kiss for everyone, with all the right additions and a reply (negative or positive, but anyway convincing) about the Guatemalan.

Now all that remains is the final part of the speech, referring to the man, which might be entitled: "What next?" Next comes the tough part, the part I have never shunned and always enjoyed. The sky has not darkened, the constellations have not fallen apart, nor have there been floods or hurricanes of extreme severity; the signs are good. They augur victory. But if they are wrong – and in the end even the gods can be wrong – I think that I'll be able to say like a poet you don't know: "I shall carry beneath the earth only the sorrow of an unfinished song." To avoid pre-mortem pathos, this letter will appear when things are really getting hot, and then you will know that your son, in a sun-drenched land of the Americas, is cursing himself for not having studied enough surgery to help a wounded man, and cursing the Mexican government that did not let him perfect his already respectable marksmanship so that he could knock over puppets with greater agility. The struggle will be with our backs to the wall, as in the hymns, until victory or death.

Again kisses, with all the affection of a farewell that refuses to be total.

Your son

Letter to his friend Tita Infante [approximately November 1956]

Dear Tita,

It's so long since I wrote to you last that I have lost the confidence which comes from regular communication (I am sure you won't understand much of my letter – I'll explain everything little by little).

First, my little Indian girl is already nine months old, quite cute, very lively, and so on.

The second and main thing is that, a while ago now, some Cuban revolutionaries asked me to help the movement with my medical "knowledge" and I accepted – because you should know the kind of work I like. I went to a ranch in the mountains to organize the physical training, to vaccinate the soldiers, etc., but I got unlucky and the police rounded everyone up. As I was not OK with my papers, I ate up a couple of months in prison; the only problem was that they stole my typewriter, among other trifles – which is the reason for this handwritten missive. Then the interior ministry made the big mistake of believing my word of honour as a gentleman and released me on condition that I leave the country within ten days. It's three months since then and I'm still around, though in hiding and without any prospects in Mexico. I'm just waiting to see what happens with the Revolution: if things go well, I'll head for Cuba; if not, I'll start looking for a country where I can camp down. This year may be a disaster in my life, but there have already been so many that it doesn't frighten me or bother me a lot.

Of course, all the scientific projects have gone to the devil and now I'm an avid reader only of Charlie and Freddie[70] and others like them. I forgot to mention that when they arrested me they found various pamphlets in Russian, as well as a card issued by the Institute for Mexican-Russian Exchange, where I had been studying the language in connection with the problem of conditioned reflexes.

Maybe it would interest you to know that my married life has almost completely broken down, and will break down for good next month when my wife goes to visit her family in Peru, from which she has been separated for the past eight years. The break-up has left a certain bitterness, because she was a loyal comrade and her revolutionary conduct was irreproachable during my forced vacations, but our minds were too far apart and I live with this anarchic spirit that dreams of new horizons as soon as I have "the cross of your arms and the land of your soul", as old Pablo said.[71]

I'll say good-bye. Don't write until you get my next letter, which will have more news or at least a settled address.

As always, a fond hug from your friend

Ernesto

---

70 Karl Marx and Friedrich Engels.
71 The reference is to Pablo Neruda's poem *Una canción desesperada*.

Appendix One

A look from the banks of the giant of rivers

Article for the Sunday supplement of *Panamá-América*, 22 November 1953

The Amazon, with its cortege of tributaries, gives shape to a huge dark continent in the centre of the Americas. During the long rainy months, all the watercourses increase their flow to such an extent that they invade the forest and convert it into an abode for creatures of the sea and air. Terrestrial animals can find refuge only on the strips of land that stick out from the dark sheet of water. Cayman, pirana and canero are the new dangerous guests of the Tronda, having replaced ocelot, jaguar and peccary in the task of preventing humans from pitching camp in the jungle.

Since those distant times when the hosts of Orellana, fearful and famished, set eyes on this muddy sea and followed it in makeshift boats to the sea, there has been endless speculation about the precise place of the giant's birth. For a long time the source was thought to be the Marañón, but modern research has shifted its attention to the other powerful tributary, the Ucayali. By patiently following its banks and breaking it down into ever smaller affluents, geographers have reached a tiny lake in the high Andes that feeds the Apurimac, at first a tinkling stream, then a powerful mountain voice, whose Quechua name translates as Great Roarer. This is where the Amazon is born.

But who here remembers the clear mountain streams – here, where the river has reached its final, colossal stature and its vast silence augments the mystery of the forest night? We are in San Pablo, a colony of patients suffering from Hansen's disease which the Peruvian government maintains on the edges of its territory and which we use as a base to enter the heart of the forest.

All representations of the forest, from Hudson's polychrome idylls to the darker tones of José E. Rivera, underestimate the smallest and most terrible enemy: the mosquito. As night falls, a shifting cloud floats over the river waters and hurls itself at any living creature that happens to be passing. It is much more dangerous to enter the forest without a mosquito net than without a weapon. Wild carnivores do not readily attack man; not all the "swamps" through which one must wade are inhabited by caymans or piranas; nor will ophidians fling themselves on a traveller to inject their poison or smother him in a deathly embrace. But mosquitoes will attack without fail. They will bite you all over your body and leave behind, instead of the blood they carry away, troublesome swellings and perhaps the yellow-fever virus or, more often, the parasite that causes malaria.

You must always descend to micro level to see the enemy. Another one, invisible and powerful, is the ancyclostoma, a parasite whose larvae penetrate the bare skin of people not wearing shoes and travel right through the body into the digestive tract, where their constant extraction of blood causes the serious anemia which, to a greater or lesser extent, affects nearly everyone in the region.

We travel through the forest, following the winding track of a native path toward the huts of the Yaguas, the indigenous inhabitants of the area. The mountain is huge and frightening: its noises and silences, its furrows of dark water or the clear drops detaching themselves from a leaf, all its well-orchestrated contradictions eventually reduce the traveller to something without magnitude or thoughts of his own. To escape this mighty influence, you have to keep your eyes on the guide's thick, sweaty neck or on the tracks imprinted in the forest floor that indicate the presence of man, so that you can remember the strength of the underlying community. When all our clothes are stuck to our bodies and water from various springs is trickling down our heads, we come upon the settlement: a small number of huts built on sticks in a forest clearing, and a thicket of manioc root (which is the

Indians' staple food here). These are ephemeral riches that will have to be abandoned when the rains swell the underground streams in the forest and drive the inhabitants into the highlands to live on the fruits of the manioc and palm harvest.

During the day, the Yaguas live in open huts with palm-leaf roofs and a platform that raises them above the ground moisture. But when night falls, the plague of mosquitoes is stronger than their stoical skin or the foul-smelling oil smeared on their bodies, and they have to take shelter in some palm-leaf huts that they hermetically seal with a door of the same material. As long as the darkness lasts, everyone remains shut up in their shelter; the promiscuous environment does not offend their sensitivities, because the moral rules by which we govern ourselves do not mean anything in the world of the tribe. I peeped in at the door of the hut and a repugnant smell of strange oils and sweaty bodies immediately drove me away.

Life for these people is reduced to following meekly the orders that nature gives them through the rain. In this winter season, they eat manioc and potatoes gathered during the summer and use their log canoes to fish in the forest swamps. It is strange to observe them: a watchful immobility that nothing disturbs, with a harpoon raised in their right hand. The dark water allows nothing to be seen; then suddenly a sharp movement sends the harpoon deep down inside it; the water becomes agitated for a moment but the only thing visible is the tiny float at one end joined to the rod by one or two metres of line. Strong paddle thrusts keep the canoe in position until the fish becomes exhausted and ceases to struggle.

When times are favourable, they also live from hunting. Occasionally they obtain a fine specimen with the help of an old shotgun they once got in exchange for something or other, but in general they prefer the silent blow-pipe. When a troop of monkeys appears among the foliage, a curare-tipped dart wounds one of them, who silently removes the encumbrance and continues on its way for a few metres until the poison takes effect and sends it crashing down, alive but unable to utter a sound. Throughout the passing of the boisterous group, the blowpipe is constantly in operation and vigilant eyes note the places where the wounded animals have fallen. When the last monkey has departed from the scene of the tragedy and no more remain to be collected, the hunters return with their contribution to the communal food supply.

In celebration of the arrival of their white visitors, they presented us with a monkey obtained in the way I have described. We rigged up a barbecue to roast the animal in the style of the Argentine pampas and tried the tough, sharp-tasting meat with its pleasantly wild fragrance. The native people were excited by our method of preparing the food.

In return for the gift, we gave them two bottles of a refreshing drink we had brought with us. The Indians eagerly drank the contents and, after a kind of religious anointing, put the tops in the plaited fibre bag around the neck which contained their most treasured possessions: an amulet, some shotgun cartridges, a seed necklace, a Peruvian sol, and so on.

As night was falling and we were worried about the return journey, one of them guided us through a number of short-cuts that got us back more quickly to the secure shelter of the metal-roofed settlement. We shook hands by way of farewell, in the European manner, and the guide gave me as a gift one of the fibres from his skirt (the only clothing worn by the Yaguas).

There has been a lot of exaggeration about the dangers and tragedies of the mountain, but one point we can confirm from our own experience. You are always warned of the perils of wandering off the beaten track in the forest, and that is correct. One day, quite close to the base we had set up, we suddenly saw to our consternation that the path we wanted to take back had faded away. We carefully retraced out steps, but to no avail. While one of us remained at a fixed place, another walked in a straight line and then guided himself back with the help of shouts. We did this, star-like, in each direction – without result. Fortunately, we had been warned in advance about such a situation and told to look for a special kind of tree whose roots form partitions several centimetres thick, sometimes jutting several metres out of the ground and seeming to give additional support to the tree.

With a normal-sized stick, we began to strike the partitions with all our might, producing a dull sound which, though not very loud, could be heard at a great distance. It is certainly much more effective than gunshot, which is smothered by the foliage. After a while, a shotgun-carrying Indian appeared with a mocking smile, led us back to the path, and pointed out the route we should have taken. Without knowing how, we had strayed off course by some 500 metres.

The forest is commonly thought to be a paradise in terms of food; it is not. A knowledgeable inhabitant will never starve to death there, but someone who carelessly got lost would face serious problems. None of the species of tropical fruit known to us grows spontaneously in the forest, and to find sustenance from the plant life one must turn to certain roots and palm fruits which only a person with experience can distinguish from poisonous types. Hunting is extremely difficult if you are not used to seeing the face of a mountain hog or other game in a split branch, or if you are not familiar with the watering places and do not know how to glide through swamps without making the slightest sound; while fishing, in a region where the density of aquatic life is so great, is nevertheless a fairly complex art because it is very unlikely that the fish will ever bite through a hook and because the harpooning method is far from simple. But agriculture: what huge pineapples! what papayas! what bananas! A little work brings handsome rewards. And yet, the spirit of the forest seems to seize its inhabitants and merge them with itself. No one works unless it is to eat. Like the monkey who scours the branches for its daily sustenance without a thought for the morrow, or like the ocelot who only kills to satisfy its need for food, the settler grows only what is necessary to avoid dying of hunger.

The days passed very quickly in the midst of scientific work, excursions and hunting parties. The time came to say goodbye, and on the night before our departure two canoe-loads of leprosy patients approached the landing stage in the healthy part of the settlement to demonstrate their affection for us. Their leonine faces were impressive to behold in the torchlit Amazonian night. A blind singer struck up some *huaynos* and *marineras*, while the motley band performed impossible feats to keep up with him. One of the patients made a farewell speech of thanks, his uncomplicated words giving off a deep emotion that blended with the imposing presence of the night. For these simple souls the mere fact of being close to them, if only out of curiosity, deserved their utmost gratitude. Expressing with grimaces the affection they could not show through a handshake (if only because the regulations categorically prohibit any contact between healthy and diseased skin), they brought to an end the serenade and the farewell. The music and the goodbyes had created a commitment towards them.

The little raft in which we were to continue our watery journey was crammed with gifts of food from the settlement staff and the patients, who vied with each other to give us the largest pineapple, the sweetest papaya, or the plumpest chicken. A little push towards the centre of the river and we were talking to it alone.

> *On the river's back*
> *comes the song of the forest*
> *comes the pain they soothe*
> *on the rafts that draw up.*
> *And the tanned boatsmen*
> *on the routes of blood*
> *of the spiralling river*
> *come drowning their sorrows.*

We had spent two days travelling downstream and were waiting to catch sight of our destination, the Colombian town of Leticia, but a serious problem arose in that we were unable to steer the unwieldy contraption. We were OK in mid-river, but whenever we tried to approach the shore for any reason we found ourselves in a furious battle with the current from which it always emerged victorious, until one of its whims allowed us to pull into whichever shore it fancied. Thus, on the evening of the third day, when the lights of the town came into view, the raft continued merrily on its way in spite of all our mighty efforts. When it seemed that our hard work was being crowned with success, the logs again pirouetted round to face the centre of the river. We kept struggling until the lights started going out upriver; we were just about to take shelter under the mosquito net, and to give up our periodical guard duty, when the last chicken (which we had been looking forward to eating) took fright and fell in the water. The current dragged it along a little more swiftly than it did ourselves. I took my clothes off and prepared to dive in; I only had to make a couple of strokes, hold out, and the raft would catch me up by itself. I don't know what happened: the night, the enigmatic river, the memory (subconscious or not) of a cayman; so the chicken kept moving on while I, furious with myself, resolved to jump in but again drew back, until I finally abandoned the enterprise. Quite frankly, the nocturnal river scared me; I was a coward in the face of nature. And afterwards we were both enormously hypocritical as we consoled each other over the dreadful fate of the poor chicken.

We woke up beached on the shore, in Brazilian territory, many hours by canoe from Leticia. But we got back there through the proverbial friendliness of the people living along the giant river.

Flying on a Colombian Army Catalina, we looked down over the immense forest. A large green cauliflower, scarcely broken by the dark thread of a broad river, stretched for thousands of kilometres and hours of flight – and even that was but a tiny part of the gigantic Amazonian continent with which we had been on such friendly terms for several months, and whose openness had us bowing in reverence.

Down below, emerging from the foliage and floating on the rivers, the spirit of Canaima, the forest god, raised his hand in farewell.

Ernesto Guevara Serna

Appendix Two

Machu-Picchu, stone enigma

Exclusive report for *Siete* by Dr Ernesto Guevara Serna (12 December 1953)

At the top of wild steep slopes, at 2,800 metres above sea level and 400 metres above the River Urubamba that bathes the heights on three sides, you meet the ancient stone city that has received the name of the place that shelters it: Machu-Picchu.

Is this its earliest name? No. The Quechua term means Old Hill, as opposed to the rocky needle rising a few metres from the town: Husina Picchu, or Young Hill – both physical descriptions simply referring to qualities of the geographical terrain. What, then, is its true name? Let us open a parenthesis and delve into the past.

The sixteenth century was a very sad time for the original inhabitants of the Americas. The bearded invaders fell like a deluge all over the continent, reducing the greater indigenous empires to rubble. In the centre of South America, internecine warfare between the two claimants to inherit Huaina-Capac's dominion, Atahualpa and Huascar, made the task of destroying the main empire on the continent much easier.

To calm the human mass that was dangerously encircling Cuzco, a decision was made that a nephew of Huascar's – the young Manco II – should become sovereign. This manoeuvre had an unexpected sequel: the indigenous peoples found themselves with a visible head, crowned according to all the formalities of Inca law possible under the Spanish yoke, and a monarch who could not be as easily manipulated as the Spanish would have wished. One night he disappeared together with his main officials, taking with him the great golden disc symbolizing the sun, and from that moment there was no peace in the old capital of the empire.

Communications were not secure. Armed bands threatened the territory and even surrounded the city itself, using as their base the imposing old fortress of Sacsahuaman (today in ruins) which guarded Cuzco. This was the year 1536.

The large-scale revolt failed, the siege of Cuzco had to be lifted, and the army of the indigenous monarch lost another major battle at Ollantaitambo, a walled city on the banks of the Urubamba. The monarch had to fall back on guerrilla warfare, which considerably harassed the Spanish rulers. Then came a day of drunkenness. A conquistador or deserter, received at the native court with six of his comrades, murdered the sovereign and was in turn – together with the other unfortunate ones – dealt a horrible death at the hands of the Indians. Their severed heads were defiantly exposed on the points of spears as a punishment and a challenge. The three sons of the sovereign – Sairy Túpac, Tito Cusi and Túpac Amaru – reigned in turn and died while still on the throne. But with the third died something more than a monarch. His passing spelt the final collapse of the Inca empire.

The ruthlessly efficient Viceroy Francisco Toledo took the last sovereign prisoner and had him executed in the Plaza de Armas in Cuzco, in 1572. In his last moments the Inca, who had reigned so briefly and whose life of confinement in the temple of the sun virgins ended so tragically, delivered a brave speech to his people which made up for his past weaknesses and led to the adoption of his name by the precursor of American independence: José Gabriel Condorcanqui, Túpac Amaru II.

The danger was over as far as the representatives of the Spanish crown were concerned, and no one thought of seeking out Vilcapampa, the well-guarded base which the last sovereign had abandoned before his capture. For three centuries the utmost silence descended on the city.

Peru remained a land largely free from European designs until an Italian scientist, Antonio Raimondi, spent 19 years of his life travelling across it in every direction during the second half of the nineteenth century. Although it is true that Raimondi was not a professional archaeologist, his profound erudition and scientific aptitude gave a huge impetus to studies of the Inca past. Guided by his monumental work, *El Perú*, generations of Peruvian students turned their gaze towards the interior of a country they barely knew, and scientists throughout the world felt a new enthusiasm for the past of a once great people.

In the early years of the twentieth century, a North American historian by the name of Professor Bingham went to Peru to study Bolívar's various itineraries on the spot and became enthralled by the extraordinary beauty of the regions he visited and the whole fascinating problem of Inca culture. Satisfying the historian and adventurer inside him, he set out to find the lost city that had been the operational base for four insurgent monarchs.

Bingham knew from the chronicles of Father Calancha and others that the Incas had had a military and political capital, which they called Vittcos, and a more remote sanctuary, Vilcapampa, where no white man had ever set foot. But for anyone who knows even a little of the region, the magnitude of the task is apparent. Entering mountainous parts covered with dense subtropical forest and criss-crossed by extremely dangerous rivers, Bingham did not know the language or even the mentality of the native inhabitants. All he had were three powerful weapons: an unquenchable thirst for adventure, a deep intuitive sense, and a good fistful of dollars.

Buying each secret or piece of information for gold, he patiently moved into the heart of the extinct civilization. Then one day in 1911, after three years of hard work, as he routinely followed an Indian who was selling a new set of stones, Bingham alone, unaccompanied by any white man, went into ecstasies at the sight of the imposing ruins surrounded and all but covered by undergrowth.

Then comes the sad part. All the ruins have been cleared of undergrowth, studied and described to perfection – but also totally stripped of anything that fell into the hands of the investigators. They triumphantly took back to their country more than two hundred crates containing priceless archaeo-logical treasures and – why not say it? – objects worth quite a lot of money. Bingham is not the guilty party; nor, objectively speaking, are the North Americans in general; and one cannot blame a government that did not have the means to fund an expedition comparable to the one organized by the discoverer of Machu-Picchu. So is no one guilty? We cannot agree with that. For where can the treasures of indigenous culture be admired or studied today? The answer is obvious: in the museums of North America.

For Bingham, Machu-Picchu was not just any discovery; it was the tri-umphant crowning of his grown-up child's dreams – for children are what all scientists of this type really are. A long series of successes and failures came to a climax here, as the stone-grey city produced visions and lucubrations propelling him into comparisons and conjectures sometimes quite remote from any empirical demonstration. The years of searching and the years following his triumph changed the itinerant historian into a learned archae-ologist, and many of his assertions, supported by the tremendous experience gained in his travels, hit the academic world with unshakeable force.

In Bingham's view, Machu-Picchu was the earliest abode of the Quechua people and the centre from which it expanded prior to the foundation of Cuzco. Bingham went deeply into Inca mythology and identified three windows of a ruined temple with the ones from which the mythical Ayullus brothers emerged; he found conclusive similarities between a circular tower in the newly rediscovered city and the temple of the sun in Cuzco; and as he conscientiously examined every possibility, he came to the conclusion that more than three centuries earlier the city had been called Vilcapampa – the sanctuary of the insurgent monarchs – and that earlier still, before the resurgence of the empire, it had been the refuge of the army of the Inca Pachacuti (whose body was kept in the city) after its defeat by Chincha troops. But in either case – refuge of conquered warriors, initial nucleus or sacred place – it turns out to have existed here at Tampu-Toco and not at

Pacaru Tampu, near Cuzco, as the Indian notables interrogated on the orders of Viceroy Toledo are said to have told the historian Sarmiento de Gamboa.

Modern researchers do not quite agree with the North American archaeologist, but they have not reached a final view about the significance of Machu-Picchu.

After several hours on board an asthmatic, almost toy-like train, which first skirted a small stream before running alongside the Urubamba, past ruins as imposing as Ollantaitambo, we finally came to the bridge across the river. A winding road then took us 400 metres above river level to the hotel of the ruins, presided over by Señor Soto, a man with exceptional knowledge of things Incan and a good singer who, on delightful tropical nights, added to the fascination of the ruined city.

Machu-Picchu is built on the crest of a hill, with a perimeter measuring two kilometres. It is divided into three sections: the temples, the main residences, and the common people's dwellings.

In the part given over to worship, one finds the huge white-granite blocks of that magnificent ruined temple whose three windows inspired Bingham's mythological speculation. Crowning a number of very finely executed buildings, Intiwatana ("the sun's mooring") is a stone finger some 60 metres high, one of the few bases for Indian ritual that survived the Spaniards' methodical destruction of that symbol as soon as they captured an Inca fortress.

The area reserved for the nobility contains exhibits of extraordinary artistic value, such as the circular tower already mentioned, a number of bridges and canals carved in stone, and many residences noteworthy for their workmanship and their stone carvings.

In marked contrast, the rocks used for the ostensibly plebeian dwellings display a characteristic lack of polish. They are separated from the religious area by a small plaza or level space, where the main reservoirs were situated, and the drying up of these sources of water is thought to have been the chief reason why the place was abandoned as a permanent settlement.

Machu-Picchu is a city of steps. Nearly all the structures are at different levels, joined by flights of steps which, whether exquisitely carved or thrown together without any aesthetic sense, are all capable of withstanding the rigours of the climate – as indeed is the whole city, which has lost only its straw and timber roofs to the elements.

Food requirements could be satisfied through vegetable-growing, on terraces that are still perfectly preserved.

The defence of the city was very simple to organize: two sides fall away almost vertically, a third is a narrow pass that can be crossed only by easily defendable paths, and a fourth is Huainca-Picchu. This peak rises some 200 metres above the level of its brother; it would be difficult to climb, almost impossible for a tourist, if remains of the Inca footpath were not still there to afford a route to the top that avoids sheer precipices. The place seems to have been used more for observation than for any other purpose, and it has no large structures. The Urubamba almost completely encircles the two hills, making it all but impossible for an attacking force to capture the site.

As we have seen, the archaeological significance of Machu-Picchu is a matter of dispute. The precise origin of the city is of little importance – or anyway, the discussion can safely be left to the experts. What is true, and important, is that it is a pure expression of the mightiest civilization in the Americas, unsullied by contact with conquering armies and filled with vast evocative treasures within its dead walls or in the fantastic surroundings. These are enough to send into ecstasies a dreamer who wanders among the ruins just for the sake of it, or a Yankee tourist loaded with practical concerns who comes across examples of the degenerate tribe and fits them in among the ancient walls, ignorant of the moral distance separating the two, because such subtleties can be appreciated only by the semi-indigenous spirit of the Latin American.

Let us agree, for now, that the city may be given two possible meanings. For the fighter pursuing what is today called a chimera, it is an arm stretched out to the future and a stony voice with continental reach; the message it shouts out is, "Citizens of Indoamerica, reconquer the past!" For others who are simply escaping "the worldly bustle", there is a sentence left in the hotel visitors' book which conveys all the bitterness of a British subject's nostalgia for empire: "I am lucky to find a place without a Coca-Cola propaganda."[72]

72 In English in the original.

Appendix Three

The dilemma of Guatemala

By Ernesto Guevara de la Serna [late 1954]

Anyone who has travelled in this part of the Americas will have heard the contemptuous words uttered about certain regimes of a clear democratic inspiration. It goes back to the idea that the Spanish Republic had been constituted by a bunch of idlers who only knew how to dance the *jota*, and that Franco had put things in order and uprooted Communism from Spain. Time subsequently polished such views and made the criteria more uniform, so that the ready-made phrase used to castigate a vanished democracy became more or less: "That wasn't liberty, it was libertinage." Such was the way of defining the governments, in Peru, Venezuela and Cuba, which gave the Americas the dream of a new era. But democratic groups in those countries had to pay a high price for the apprenticeship in techniques of repression, as numerous innocent victims were sacrificed to maintain an order necessary to the interests of the feudal bourgeoisie and foreign capital. Patriots know today that victory will be conquered with blood and fire, that there can be no pardon for the traitors, that total extermination of the reactionary groups is the only way of ensuring the rule of justice in the Americas.

When I again heard the word "libertinage" to describe Guatemala, I felt fearful for that small republic. Is the dream of Latin Americans, now reincarnated in Guatemala and Bolivia, doomed to follow the path of its predecessors? This is where the dilemma is posed.

Four revolutionary parties form the base of the government, and all of them – except the PGT – are divided into two or more factions which fight among themselves more furiously than against the traditional feudal enemies, forgetting in their own dissensions the real objective of Guatemalans. Meanwhile, reaction lays its snares. The US State Department and the United Fruit Company – one never quite knows which is which in that land to the north – have formed an open alliance with the landowners and the God-fearing bourgeoisie and assorted holy Joes; they have made all kinds of plans to silence the insolent enemy who has sprung up in the bosom of the Caribbean. While Caracas waits for reports to serve as the pretext for more or less brazen interference, displaced generals and frightened coffee growers are seeking to link up with sinister neighbouring dictators.

While the muzzled press of bordering countries is allowed only one tone in which to sing the praises of the "leader", here the self-styled "independent" papers are unleashing a tempest of crude lies about the government and its supporters, in order to create the sought-after climate. And democracy allows this.

The "Communist beachhead", giving a magnificent example of liberty and ingenuity, is allowing its nationalist cement to be undermined; it is allowing another dream of the Americas to be destroyed.

Look a little at the recent past, comrades, at the fugitive, dead or captured leaders of APRA in Peru or Acción Democrática in Venezuela, at the magnificent Cuban escapade struck down by Batista. Peep into the 20 orifices in the body of the soldier-poet Ruiz Pineda, or the miasmal prisons of Venezuela. Behold these examples fearlessly but warily and answer whether this is the future of Guatemala.

Is this what the struggle has been for? The people who are achieving the hopes of Latin America bear a great responsibility. It is time to do away with euphemisms. It is time to answer the garrotte with the garrotte – and if it is necessary to die, let it be in the manner of Sandino not Azaña. But let not the treacherous rifles be wielded by Guatemalans. If they want to murder liberty, let them do it themselves – those who hide it. One must not be meek and mild, must not forgive betrayals. Let not the unshed blood of one traitor cost the blood of thousands of brave defenders of the people. Hamlet's old disjunction resonates on my lips through a poet of the Americas – Guatemala: "Are you or are you not, or who are you?" The groups supporting the government have the word.

BACK ON THE ROAD

Ernesto Guevara (he was always known by the Argentine nickname 'Che') was born in Rosario, Argentina, in 1928 and trained as a doctor. Disillusioned with the right-wing government of Juan Perón, he left home and, in 1959, he helped Fidel Castro to overthrow the Cuban dictator Batista. He was a minister in the Cuban government from 1961 to 1965 and became a key figure in the revolutionary movements on the 1960s. He was killed in Bolivia in 1967.

Richard Gott was for many years the *Guardian*'s correspondent in Latin America. He met 'Che' Guevara in Cuba in 1963, later reported from Bolivia during his campaign there in 1967, and was present in Valegrande on the day of his death. He is the author of *Guerrilla Movements in Latin America* (1971), *Land Without Evil* (1991) and *In the Shadow of the Liberator* (2000).

Patrick Camiller has translated from several European languages. Spanish-language titles include novels by Manuel Vásquez Montalban, Adolfo Gilly's *The Mexican Revolution* and 'Che' Guevara's Congo diaries, *The African Dream*.

ALSO BY ERNESTO 'CHE' GUEVARA

The African Dream
The Diaries of the Revolutionary
War in the Congo
The Motorcycle Diaries